Up-Side-Down Gospel!

Wasn't the <u>world</u> going to get turned upside-down?

Samuel Ross

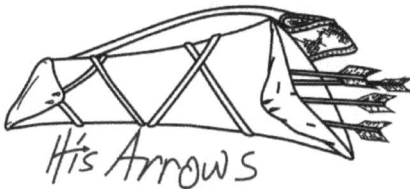

His Arrows Publishing

Second Printing, 2014

Published by His Arrows Publishing Company
Facebook: https://www.facebook.com/profile.php?id=100004266946362
e-mail: samuelross2003@gmail.com

ISBN: 978-0692260203

Printed in the United States of America

Front and back cover original photography by Justin.
Back cover and interior original artwork by Jordan.

All Scripture quotes are taken from the Holy Bible, King James Version.

"He that hath my commandments, and keepeth them, he it is that loveth me: and he that loveth me shall be loved of my Father, and I will love him, and will manifest myself to him." John 14:21

In Appreciation:

There are several people who share the credit for seeing this book finished. Thank you to my son Jordan who provided the initial critique and review for his generation. Thank you to my friends Jim C and Tim B who provided feedback and edits, for our generation. Thank you to my son Justin, who provided his talent for adding "flow"...

And thank you to my wife Michelle, who was my main editor, supporter and encourager through the process. Finally, I owe much of my desire to take on this project to my earthly Father, who spent many years as a prayer intercessor for his children, before joining our Heavenly Father three years ago. Thank you for loving me!

Dedication:

I dedicate this book to my four sons. It is my deepest desire that they know their Heavenly Father on this side of Heaven better than they have known me.

Foreword:

My reason for writing this book is to provide a perspective of the Gospel that will help to set a few things upright that have been flipped topsy-turvy. In doing so, what I share is the truth that I found which set me free. Free from misbeliefs.

God wants us all to be free! Jesus bled and died so we <u>can</u> be free and He deserves what He paid for!

God gave us a book to introduce us to Himself. That book, the Bible, wasn't meant to be complicated. In fact, He has given us His Holy Spirit with the mission of teaching us what the Bible means. In doing this, He has ensured that we can understand His book no matter how complicated mankind may make it appear.

No single book, no matter how large, can completely explain God. As we listen and draw closer to God, He will show us what we've been searching for. He will open up greater understanding of His ways and His love to us.

(Note: The King James Version of the Holy Bible is used for all Scripture quotes in this book, for the sake of consistency. Feel free to follow along in your favorite Bible translation.)

Table of Contents:

Foreword

Introduction

Afterword

Introduction: How can we know whether what we believe is really true?

If you believed a lie, how would you know? Is there someone you would trust to tell you? How can you be sure they know the truth on the subject? How can you know if what you think about the Bible is true?

What if what we "think" we know (those things we've decided to believe) are not based on truth? What if there's more "tradition" than truth in what we've learned about the Bible because we didn't go to the source? This was the problem that Jesus was pointing out when He said, "Ye have heard that it hath been said, An eye for an eye, and a tooth for a tooth: But I say unto you, That ye resist not evil: but whosoever shall smite thee on thy right cheek, turn to him the other also. And if any man will sue thee at the law, and take away thy coat, let him have thy cloak also. And whosoever shall compel thee to go a mile, go with him twain. Give to him that asketh thee, and from him that would borrow of thee turn not thou away." (Matthew 5:38-42) Religious people in Jesus' day had decided to apply their own meaning in their lives for many of the Old Testament passages. Jesus was straightening out their misbeliefs.

Does the Bible tell us to get our understanding from other people? What would happen if we checked out the Bible for ourselves to see what it says? Could we understand it for ourselves? Did God provide any help in this?

Let's take a look at the topic of "faith" as an example of what can happen if we let other people tell us what the Bible says. We are told we must "walk by faith…" when we ask for explanations of the parts of the Bible that are difficult to understand. What if walking by faith doesn't mean to accept things blindly? What if there's substance to faith?

When the people in the Bible believed by faith (including acting on it), God showed up and their faith resulted in changes, blessings, and even miracles! What does this faith look like? Faith that the Bible speaks about is not blindly following something we hear or read with no hope of seeing what that faith is based on. Hebrews 11:1 says: "Now faith is the substance of things hoped for, the evidence of things not seen." So, faith is substance and evidence, both words that express proof. The confidence and assurance we have is what God has told us! Biblical faith is: believing what God has told you. This word "believe" is not referring to accepting an idea or giving mental agreement to a theology.

One of the dictionary definitions for believe is "to hold as an opinion." This is not what the Bible is talking about! The Greek word used in the New Testament that is translated "believe" means: to commit to, to place trust in, and by implication to entrust your spiritual well-being to Christ. So, to believe in Him is to place your trust and confidence fully in God, Jesus and the Holy Spirit!

How important is it to believe what He tells us? Matthew records, "But he answered and said, It is written, Man shall not live by bread alone, but by every word that proceedeth out of the mouth of God." (Matthew 4:4) Believing what He tells us is essential for life! Notice that Jesus was NOT talking about the words that are written in the Bible when He said, "...every word that comes from the mouth of God." The Bible does not contain "every word" from God's mouth. Even John pointed this out in the last chapter of the Gospel account he wrote. "And there are also many other things which Jesus did, the which, if they should be written every one, I suppose that even the world itself could not contain the books that should be written. Amen."

The Greek word translated "word" in Matthew 4:4 is "Rhema." Rhema means an utterance from God directed to us and proceeding = now, so it is the words we receive from Him now! So, my question to you is this – Do you believe the Bible or your experience (or in this case, lack of experience)? If the Bible says we need

God's words to us now for life, then we would be missing something without them. And there is much more in the Bible on this subject.

Jesus said, "...I am come that they might have life, and that they might have it more abundantly." This is the life we can only receive through the proceeding words direct from God. This is not "surviving." This is living! Jesus also pointed out that His sheep hear His voice (John 10). If we're His sheep then He says we hear His voice. Maybe the issue is that without His help we just don't recognize His voice.

Jesus also said, "...he hath anointed me to preach the gospel to the poor; he hath sent me to heal the brokenhearted, to preach deliverance to the captives..." (Luke 4) And He said, "If the Son therefore shall make you free, ye shall be free indeed." (John 8:36) If you have not experienced this life, this freedom, then it may be that you've believed man instead of God, in regards to Jesus' promises.

Would you like to know what His life looks like? Would you like to know what true freedom feels like? Then read on. This book was written for you!

God wants us to know the truth – the truth about Him and the truth about ourselves. From Genesis, Chapter 3, it is apparent that our mutual enemy does not want us to know the truth. So, it is imperative that we learn how to find truth and where to look. Jesus gave us perhaps the most focused clue that we have in the Bible about this, when He said, "I am the way, the truth, and the life: no man cometh unto the Father, but by me." God also gave us this promise, "And ye shall seek me, and find me, when ye shall search for me with all your heart." (Jeremiah 29)

In a world where many voices claim to have all the answers and "the way," how can we know who will tell us the truth? Fortunately, Jesus gave us the answer to this in a promise: "Howbeit when he, the Spirit of truth, is come, he will guide you into all truth: for he shall not speak of himself; but whatsoever he shall hear, that shall he speak: and he will shew you things to come." (John 16:13)

If Holy Spirit is our guide to find "all truth" then how much truth does that leave us to find from other sources? We can certainly listen to other people and learn a lot from them, as well as read great writings by gifted authors. The possibilities are endless. But, in terms of knowing the truth, when someone tells us what they believe all we can know for sure is that they believe it. God is the source of all truth and He has given us His Spirit to make sure we can find the way.

Let's look at this in another way. If your best friend was in a tough situation and you wanted to find out what happened so you could help, who would you ask? Would you go to their spouse? Or their neighbor? Or another mutual friend? Perhaps the mailman? Or a coffee barista? Who would you really go to, if you wanted the whole story, all the facts? Who else could possibly give it to you in full detail but your friend, the person who was experiencing tough times? Likewise, how can we be sure that what we believe about God is true without getting it straight from Him?

When it comes to reading the Bible, and it is very important that we do so, can we be sure that we understand it correctly as we read? If we read a dozen commentaries can we know that those writers had the correct translations? No, we need His Holy Spirit to provide understanding. Our part is to read the Bible, to take in what He has provided for us. His part is to illuminate it so that we understand it. We can trust His promises that He will do this for us.

Traditional teaching about how to study the Bible focuses on studying to find out how we're supposed to live/act. We're told that the Bible will teach us what the rules are that we must live by. But the Bible was written as an introduction to God. What would happen if we studied it to learn what He is like, how He speaks and how He works? This would result in us learning how to interact with Him! This is what He has invited us to.

Perhaps we should take the New Covenant seriously: "For this is the covenant that I will make with the house of Israel after those days, saith the Lord; I will put my laws into their mind, and write them in their hearts: and I will be to them a God, and they shall be to me a people: And they shall not teach every man his neighbour, and every man his brother, saying, Know the Lord: for all shall know me, from the least to the greatest. For I will be merciful to their unrighteousness, and their sins and their iniquities will I remember no more." (Hebrews 8:10-12)

Chapter 1 - When did God stop communicating with His children?

Allegory - I have a good friend who was born into a unique circumstance. When he was born, both of his parents worked and so neither one had much time for him. They left him at daycare all day and even in the evening when he was at home they didn't spend hardly any time with him (okay, maybe his situation wasn't totally unique...). In fact, he didn't hear his parents talk after he was about one and a half years old, at all. As he learned how to talk at the daycare, he really wanted to talk to his parents. When he tried talking with them, they sometimes looked at him and smiled or nodded their heads, so he realized that they could hear him. Yet, they never spoke to him. They were just too busy with work and other activities they had to do.

One day he explained what it was like at home to one of the teachers at the daycare. This person told him,

"You silly boy, your parents can't talk!" So, my friend just accepted that idea and went on to live his life having never heard his parents talk throughout his childhood and into adulthood.

Unfortunately, this situation had dire consequences. He never learned anything directly from his parents. He never knew what they really believed. He never heard about their lives. He never knew what their dreams were for him. He never knew whether they liked his choice of a school to go to, or the woman he married. He never really knew if they liked his children, although they did send them presents on their birthdays and at Christmas.

All throughout his life he met other people who had a similar experience to his, so it seemed inescapable to him. Oddly, his parents weren't the only ones who never spoke to him. Their lifestyles seemed to rub off on his older brother, who never spoke to him either.

Then one day when he was nearly 40 years old, my friend's Father called him up and told him, "I just found out today that one of your daycare teachers told you that your Mother and I can't talk. I wanted you to know that this isn't true. In fact, we talked to you almost continually when you were growing up, and we wondered why you almost never responded to us. We thought something might be wrong with your speech development, but then watched as you interacted with your friends. It broke our hearts that you didn't want to talk with us, but we just decided to accept it and love you anyway."

Thus began an amazing journey for my friend, when as an adult he was able to become true friends with his parents and with his brother as well. This journey has continued for over 15 years now, every day filled with surprises, as he finds out something else new about them and he sees his relationship with them grow.

How would you feel if this happened to you? What would you do if you saw friends of yours do this to their child? Doesn't it just seem outrageous?! Wouldn't you speak up and try to correct the situation? Well, the story I just told you is real. It's about my relationship with My Heavenly Father, His Holy Spirit, and Jesus.

And it may be true for you as well. You see, I was taught at a very early age that God doesn't speak to His children any more. And since I didn't know what His voice sounded like and the people who told me this were very trustworthy, I believed them. When I heard a voice (in my mind) that I didn't understand, I wrote it off as my imagination or sub-conscious mind. Then one day I read a book by an author who knew that God indeed does still speak to His children. When I accepted this fact as truth, and asked God to help me hear Him, I began to recognize His voice. Since that time, I've come to learn a lot more about Him that I wasn't taught in my youth.

If we believe that God created us in His image, then why do we accept that God stopped talking to His children? As parents, would we ever imagine not talking to our young children? (If you're not a parent, no worries, you know the answer to this from your own childhood!)

In order to make sure we understand that He loves us, God has put a lot of emphasis on communicating with us. He gave us the Bible, which is quite a large book actually, through a number of authors. He made sure this book tells us just how important He feels communication is. And nowhere in this book does it say He is ever going to stop!

In the Old Testament God asks us over and over to listen to His voice. For example: "And said, If thou wilt diligently hearken to the voice of the LORD thy God, and wilt do that which is right in his sight, and wilt give ear to his commandments, and keep all his statutes, I will put none of these diseases upon thee, which I have brought upon the Egyptians: for I am the LORD that healeth thee." (Exodus

15:26) And, "Hear, O Israel: The LORD our God is one LORD:" (Deuteronomy 6:4)

He also made it plain to the Children of Israel that He wanted them to communicate directly with Him, rather than through someone else. This is part of a close, intimate relationship with someone. In Exodus the LORD said to Moses, "And the LORD said unto Moses, Go unto the people, and sanctify them today and tomorrow, and let them wash their clothes, And be ready against the third day: for the third day the LORD will come down in the sight of all the people upon mount Sinai. And Moses brought forth the people out of the camp to meet with God; and they stood at the nether part of the mount." (Exodus 19:10-11&17)

In the New Testament, Jesus explained that He is the "Good Shepherd" (John 10) and told His followers that His sheep hear His voice and follow Him because they know His voice. What does that mean for people who believe they know God but don't hear His voice?

Jesus also pointed out, when being tempted by the enemy, that we can only truly live by the words that come to us directly from God!" (Matthew 4) Yet many Christians are not aware of God speaking to them. Perhaps that's why the Old Testament prophet Hosea recorded God's statement, "My people are destroyed for lack of knowledge…"

Now, if God just stopped at "speaking" then His communication with us might not be very effective. This is because He made us in such a way that we learn much better when things are demonstrated. So, wouldn't it just be like God to want to demonstrate things to us so that we would really know and understand what He is telling us? This is very important for a couple of reasons. First, to "know" God is to receive understanding through experience and He wants us to know Him. Second, our faith is increased every time we experience Him. And indeed, this approach is exactly what we see in many, many examples in the Bible.

We could look at a myriad of people, to draw examples, but here are just a few. Abraham was called by God and told to leave the land of his Father and go to a place God would show him. God did not tell him where He would take Abraham, just asked him to obey and then learn by "walking it out." He also told Abraham that he would have a son and be the Father of many nations. But it then took 25 years before that son was born. God was teaching Abraham how to be the Father that Isaac needed. Abraham learned by experiencing it. This learning included making more than just a few mistakes!

Isaac was told by God to stay in the land of Canaan (Genesis 26), when there was drought and it appeared that everyone would starve. In fact, others were leaving the area. But God told Isaac that He would provide for him and prosper him. Isaac stayed, planted a crop, and he was rewarded with a 100-fold increase in his harvest! He learned through experience that God is indeed the Provider (Jehovah Jireh), as he promised.

Noah was told by God to build a boat. Imagine being told that water was going to fall from the sky and cause a great flood, if you had never seen rain before! Noah obeyed God, to build the boat, a task that took 100 years. In doing this, he came to know God (through experience), as his protector.

Here's a real-life example of how we need to experience something to really know it, that we all can relate to. Before we ever tried driving a car, most of us rode in cars with other people driving. In most cases, we even thought that we knew how to drive before we were old enough and before we were given the chance to try. We also heard a lot about driving and if we took a "Driver's Training" course, we also read a lot about it. However, only when we actually got behind the wheel of a car, started it, and drove it out into the street did we finally actually "learn" how to drive. This is when we finally began to "see" the real dangers and risks that are there, as well as how important it is to keep our eyes on the road (well at least for some of us...).

In the New Testament Jesus even tells us, with a promise, that He will help us learn in this same manner. In the book of John, He says, "He that hath my commandments, and keepeth them, he it is that loveth me: and he that loveth me shall be loved of my Father, and I will love him, and will manifest myself to him." (John 14:21) He promises that in return for obeying whatever He has told us to do, He will manifest Himself to us (to show us who He is in a tangible way)! In this way, we get to experience Him as well as receive confirmation that we heard correctly.

God points out in the Bible that He doesn't change. Should we believe people who say that God has stopped speaking to people today (because they haven't heard Him) or should we believe the Bible?

Consider this. If we can hear God and Jesus speaking to us, then we don't need to rely on other people as our source for knowing what God has to say. Instead, we can check with those who also hear Him, for confirmation of what He has told us. He has promised to reveal the truth to us directly and individually.

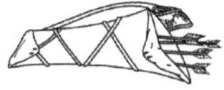

Chapter 2 - How does God "speak" to us?

How would you go about trying to find out what your favorite celebrity or hero is really like? Would you go to someone who has never even met them? How about if you wanted to know what food from another country tasted like? Would you ask a person who has only ever eaten American food what the food in Thailand tastes like? No?

When we want to know about God and His love letter to us, the Bible, wouldn't it make sense to seek out people who believe God is speaking to His children today and who are experiencing His work in their lives daily?

When your spouse or best friend wants you to know that they don't agree with a statement you have made, do they always use words to tell you or do they sometimes just "give you that look..."? When your child does something that really makes you proud, can't they see by the look on your face how pleased you are with them, even before you speak to them? Don't we all have a myriad of facial expressions that we use every day to communicate to other people how we feel? We can also expect that God will use many other means of communication besides just verbal!

Interestingly, when expressing that God communicated with someone, many passages in the Bible just say, "... and God spoke to _____." (fill in the blank). This leaves it open for people to assume a variety of things about what "God spoke" actually looks like. When I was young, I thought this meant that He walked up to them, stood face to face with them, and looked them right in the eye. Of course, the Bible gives us many clues and facts about how He speaks, with several detailed accounts. For instance, Deuteronomy states, "And there arose not a prophet since in Israel like unto Moses, whom the LORD knew face to face..." (34:10)

Aaron and Miriam had this encounter with God: "And the LORD came down in the pillar of the cloud, and stood in the door of the tabernacle, and called Aaron and Miriam: and they both came forth. And he said, Hear now my words: If there be a prophet among you, I the LORD will make myself known unto him in a vision, and will speak unto him in a dream. My servant Moses is not so, who is faithful in all mine house. With him will I speak mouth to mouth, even apparently, and not in dark speeches; and the similitude of the LORD shall he behold: wherefore then were ye not afraid to speak against my servant Moses?" (Numbers 12:5-8) It seems that God has many different ways of speaking with people!

Abraham experienced God in this manner: "And the LORD said, Shall I hide from Abraham that thing which I do...?" (Genesis 18:17) And the LORD said, "Because the cry of Sodom and Gomorrah is great, and because their sin is very grievous; I will go down now, and see whether they have done altogether according to the cry of it, which is come unto me; and if not, I will know." And the men turned their faces from thence, and went toward Sodom: but Abraham stood yet before the LORD. And Abraham drew near, and said, "Wilt thou also destroy the righteous with the wicked?" (Genesis 18:20-23)

God appeared to Abraham and spoke with him face to face. What Abraham experienced was three men standing in front of him.

The New Testament tells us, "God, who at sundry times and in divers manners spake in time past unto the fathers by the prophets, Hath in these last days spoken unto us by his Son, whom he hath appointed heir of all things, by whom also he made the worlds..." (Hebrews 1:1-2)

While God used His prophets to speak to many people in the past (Old Covenant times), He sent Jesus to speak to us directly. This is an important shift because God used to speak to a Prophet and have them tell people what He was saying. This was the only way that most people heard from God back then. However, when Jesus came, God made some changes that mean we no longer need someone else to hear Him for us and tell us what He is saying. First, He chose to speak to mankind directly through Jesus. Second, He gave His Holy Spirit to us in order to speak to the whole world. We will touch more on this subject later.

Jesus also tells us that His sheep hear His voice in John 10. So we know that we can expect to be hearing from Him in some manner. We are told in the New Testament that the Holy Spirit is inside of us. So it seems apparent that we should expect His voice or "directions" to come from inside.

You may be asking, "But what does this "sound" like?" As it turns out, you already hear that sound! And, so does the rest of the world, believers as well as pre-believers.

This may be a surprising claim to you, so let me provide an illustration to support it. In some of the old classical movies, as well as more recent cartoons, it has been popular to depict when a person is going through an internal struggle by showing a small angel on one of the person's shoulders and a small devil on the other shoulder, each whispering into the respective ears. These two apparitions will each have the face of the person they are trying to persuade. In most of the movies where this type of scene is used, it is done for comedic relief.

Consider for a moment why this works. Why is it funny? Why do people "get" the joke? Why do they use the face of the person on the angel and devil? Well, the answer is that everyone can identify with hearing that internal struggle of two voices – one which is arguing to do the "right thing" and one which is arguing to just have fun or go "do your own thing." But where are those voices coming from? Most people probably assume the voices are their conscience on the one shoulder and their real desires/will on the other shoulder, or something similar. In fact, this is even taught.

I will suggest, with Biblical support, that it is actually the Holy Spirit and a messenger of satan that are the voices we hear, most of the time. One reason for saying that the positive voice is not us talking is the passage in the Bible that explains there is no good in man. This makes it kind of tough to support that the "good voice" is some part of me, such as subconscious thoughts. In fact, I will point out that what the world calls conscience, Christians should understand to be

God's Spirit! Jesus stated that after He was gone God would send His Holy Spirit to convict the world of: sin, righteousness and judgment. (John 16:7-11) Everyone in the world hears Him on these three things. Do you know what your conscience sounds like? Then you know what He sounds like when He speaks directly to you, from His Spirit to yours.

Here's a Bible passage that expresses His voice in this way. The prophet Elijah was up on a mountain and God spoke to Him. "And he said, Go forth, and stand upon the mount before the LORD. And, behold, the LORD passed by, and a great and strong wind rent the mountains, and brake in pieces the rocks before the LORD; but the LORD was not in the wind: and after the wind an earthquake; but the LORD was not in the earthquake: And after the earthquake a fire; but the LORD was not in the fire: and after the fire a still small voice" (1Kings 19:11-12)

Have you heard His still small voice? This is perhaps the most common way we will hear God, if we are listening and expecting to hear Him. However, when we don't know this is Him speaking we are likely to chalk this up to our conscience, an impression, or our sub-conscious thoughts.

Jesus explained that His Spirit would be speaking to us when He described the Spirit's role, "And I will pray the

Father, and he shall give you another Comforter, that he may abide with you for ever; Even the Spirit of truth; whom the world cannot receive, because it seeth him not, neither knoweth him: but ye know him; for he dwelleth with you, and shall be in you. But the Comforter, which is the Holy Ghost, whom the Father will send in my name, he shall teach you all things, and bring all things to your remembrance, whatsoever I have said unto you." (John 14:16-17 & 26)

And, "Howbeit when he, the Spirit of truth, is come, he will guide you into all truth: for he shall not speak of himself; but whatsoever he shall hear, that shall he speak: and he will shew you things to come. He shall glorify me: for he shall receive of mine, and shall shew it unto you." (John 16:13-14)

It is important to catch the fact that Jesus promised that the Holy Spirit will be communicating with us. He even told His disciples that it is better for us that He, Jesus, goes away so that the Father would send His Holy Spirit!

Notice in this passage, John 16, the use of the word "all." The Greek word used for all, *pas*, has a rather unique meaning. It simply means "all" or "the whole" and nothing less. When Jesus says that the Holy Spirit will teach us all things and guide us into all truth how much does that leave for us to get from other sources? (I'll cover more on this topic in a later chapter.) Chapter 16 also points out that the Holy Spirit convicts the world, the whole world. It is apparent that He is talking to everyone. Some Christians struggle with this idea. It is very clear here!

Then there's that other voice, that guy sitting on the other shoulder and coaxing us to follow our own desires. Some people, perhaps most, just figure that this is our sinful nature coming out. Look what Jesus had to say about him: "...He was a murderer from the beginning, and abode not in the truth, because there is no truth in him. When he speaketh a lie, he speaketh of his own: for he is a liar, and the father of it." (John 8:44b) That voice couldn't tell you the truth if it wanted to!

Consider what Paul had to say about the way the enemy of our souls tries to fight against us, through our thoughts: "For the weapons of our warfare are not carnal, but mighty through God to the pulling down of strong holds; Casting down imaginations, and every high thing that exalteth itself against the knowledge of God, and bringing into captivity every thought to the obedience of Christ..." (2Corinthians 10:4-5)

Indeed, any argument or pretense that is against what God is telling us is from our mutual enemy. That is exactly what that other voice whispering in our ear is doing, arguing with the Holy Spirit of God! This reveals the fact that spiritual attacks take place in our minds.

That is where the battle is. The fight is focused on who we believe, God or the enemy!

I find it amazing that the secular world comes so close to getting this correct, with images comfortable to them, the depiction of an angel and a devil. Meanwhile, many if not most Christians aren't even aware that this spiritual struggle is going on!

God also still speaks to us in an audible voice at times. This may be experienced less frequently for most people. However there are multiple instances of this happening in the New Testament with Jesus' disciples. It happened with Paul, in Acts 9.

Speaking is not the only way God communicates with us. I chose to focus on the ways that He "speaks" to us in this Chapter because the Bible provides the most specific information about this form of communication. There are other ways that He communicates with us. For instance, there are many stories of God using dreams to speak to His children in the Bible and those dreams were life-changing for those people. It is obvious that they took the dreams seriously!

Perhaps He uses dreams, while we are asleep, because it is almost the only time He can get our undivided attention. Since the Holy Spirit is inside of us and is dwelling in the heart of our being, literally our bowels, He can also communicate to us in ways that feel very similar to our emotions (like joy, sadness, etc.). Paul mentions that He is interceding with God for us: "Likewise the Spirit also helpeth our infirmities: for we know not what we should pray for as we ought: but the Spirit itself maketh intercession for us with groanings which cannot be uttered." (Romans 8:26) We will sometimes feel these groans, mentally or physically, and may even join Him in praying. Once we begin to expect to hear Him, He will show us other ways that He uses to get our attention.

Chapter 3 - What is God's purpose for providing the Bible?

God has provided us with a history (His story) of how and why He placed mankind on earth. In this book He explains who He is and what His character is like. He has preserved this book, ensuring that it would survive for several millennia so far. Some parts have been preserved longer than others. There are many clues to God's purpose for the Bible provided within some of the major stories. Here are a few examples.

God gave a set of instructions to Moses for His people that came with a command that they be written down. And He actually wrote them Himself: "And the LORD said unto Moses, Come up to me into the mount, and be there: and I will give thee tables of stone, and a law, and commandments which I have written; that thou mayest teach them." (Exodus 24:12) "And he gave unto Moses, when he had made an end of communing with him upon mount Sinai, two tables of testimony, tables of stone, written with the finger of God." (Exodus 31:18)

When giving the terms of the Law to Moses, God gave him these instructions for kings whom He would choose to rule over the people: "And it shall be, when he sitteth upon the throne of his kingdom, that he shall write him a copy of this law in a book out of that which is before the priests the Levites: And it shall be with him, and he shall read therein all the days of his life: that he may learn to fear the LORD his God, to keep all the words of this law and these statutes, to do them: That his heart be not lifted up above his brethren, and that he turn not aside from the commandment, to the right hand, or to the left: to the end that he may prolong his days in his kingdom, he, and his children, in the midst of Israel." (Deuteronomy 17:18-20)

And, God gave Joshua instructions pertaining to His book as well: "This book of the law shall not depart out of thy mouth; but thou shalt meditate therein day and night, that thou mayest observe to do according to all that is written therein: for then thou shalt make thy way prosperous, and then thou shalt have good success." (Joshua 1:8)

So, God gave His people the book of the Law, to protect them from disobedience and disbelief. Then, in the New Testament we are given further explanation of the purpose of the Law: "Therefore by the deeds of the law there shall no flesh be justified in his sight: for by the law is the knowledge of sin." (Romans 3:20) "What shall we say then? Is the law sin? God forbid. Nay, I had not known sin, but by the law: for I had not known lust, except the law had said, Thou shalt not covet." (Romans 7:7)

So, the law was given that mankind might know what sin is. And, Paul further explains that the Law had an even greater purpose:

"Brethren, I speak after the manner of men; Though it be but a man's covenant, yet if it be confirmed, no man disannulleth, or addeth thereto. Now to Abraham and his seed were the promises made. He saith not, And to seeds, as of many; but as of one, And to thy seed, which is Christ. And this I say, that the covenant, that was confirmed before of God in Christ, the law, which was four hundred and thirty years after, cannot disannul, that it should make the promise of none effect. For if the inheritance be of the law, it is no more of promise: but God gave it to Abraham by promise. Wherefore then serveth the law? It was added because of transgressions, till the seed should come to whom the promise was made; and it was ordained by angels in the hand of a mediator. Now a mediator is not a mediator of one, but God is one. Is the law then against the promises of God? God forbid: for if there had been a law given which could have given life, verily righteousness should have been by the law. But the scripture hath concluded all under sin, that the promise by faith of Jesus Christ might be given to them that believe. But before faith came, we were kept under the law, shut up unto the faith which should afterwards be revealed. Wherefore the law was our schoolmaster to bring us unto Christ, that we might be justified by faith. But after that faith is come, we are no longer under a schoolmaster. For ye are all the children of God by faith in Christ Jesus." (Galatians 3:15-26)

To summarize what Paul revealed in this passage: The original covenant with Abraham pre-dated the Law. Therefore the Law did not change that covenant. That covenant promised a Messiah who would rule forever (which requires that He defeat satan). But, the Law was a guardian for mankind until the Messiah, Jesus, came! Now that He is here, we no longer need this guardian over us, because faith is here! No one was able to keep all of the Law all of the time. The Law served to show mankind that we cannot live up to God's standard on our own. This emphasizes why we needed Jesus' sacrifice. His sacrifice fulfilled the Law, so we don't have to. Now that's good news!

Another historical fact that Paul reveals is the purpose of recording some of the history of the Israelites: "These things happened to them as examples and were written down as warnings for us, on whom the culmination of the ages has come." (1Corinthians 10:11) God wanted us to have written instructions, recorded to teach us!

When giving instructions on the purpose of scripture, Paul told Timothy, "All scripture is given by inspiration of God, and is profitable for doctrine, for reproof, for correction, for instruction in righteousness: That the man of God may be perfect, thoroughly furnished unto all good works." (2 Timothy 3:16-17) What was Paul referring to when he used the word scripture? The Old Testament, as we call it, was all that they had at the time. The New Testament is a collection of letters that were written after Jesus was here on earth and then gathered together many years later.

John, when explaining why he wrote the Gospel account that bears his name, stated: "And many other signs truly did Jesus in the presence of his disciples, which are not written in this book: But these are written, that ye might believe that Jesus is the Christ, the Son of God; and that believing ye might have life through his name." (John 20:30-31)

In the book of Revelation, John explains that he was told to write down what he was shown in a series of visions. He didn't know that these writings would become a part of our modern Bible at the time, but God certainly did.

All throughout the Bible God explains (and promises) who He is and what He will do for those who have believed Him and will obey Him. To Abraham He said, "And I will establish my covenant between me and thee and thy seed after thee in their generations for an everlasting covenant, to be a God unto thee, and to thy seed after thee." (Genesis

17:7) **To Jacob He said,** "And he said, I am God, the God of thy father: fear not to go down into Egypt; for I will there make of thee a great nation..." **(Genesis 46:3)**

To Moses and the Children of Israel He said, "Wherefore say unto the children of Israel, I am the LORD, and I will bring you out from under the burdens of the Egyptians, and I will rid you out of their bondage, and I will redeem you with a stretched out arm, and with great judgments: And I will take you to me for a people, and I will be to you a God: and ye shall know that I am the LORD your God, which bringeth you out from under the burdens of the Egyptians.'" **(Exodus 6:6-7)**

To Joshua, after he became the leader of Israel when Moses died, He said, "Have not I commanded thee? Be strong and of a good courage; be not afraid, neither be thou dismayed: for the LORD thy God is with thee whithersoever thou goest." **(Joshua 1:9) To David He said,** "I will declare the decree: the LORD hath said unto me, Thou art my Son; this day have I begotten thee. Ask of me, and I shall give thee the heathen for thine inheritance, and the uttermost parts of the earth for thy possession." **(Psalms 2:7-8)**

In the lives of these Old Testament Patriarchs mentioned, it becomes clear that they had close relationships with God. They spoke with Him and discussed real issues with Him on a regular basis.

When Jesus came, He showed that He was the Messiah that was promised, the fulfillment of prophesy! "From that time Jesus began to preach, and to say, 'Repent: for the kingdom of heaven is at hand.'" (Matthew 4:17)

"When the even was come, they brought unto him many that were possessed with devils: and he cast out the spirits with his word, and healed all that were sick: That it might be fulfilled which was spoken by Esaias the prophet, saying, 'Himself took our infirmities, and bare our sicknesses.'" (Matthew 8:16-17)

"Now after that John was put in prison, Jesus came into Galilee, preaching the gospel of the kingdom of God, And saying, The time is fulfilled, and the kingdom of God is at hand: repent ye, and believe the gospel.'" (Mark 1:14-15)

"And he came to Nazareth, where he had been brought up: and, as his custom was, he went into the synagogue on the sabbath day, and stood up for to read. And there was delivered unto him the book of the prophet Esaias. And when he had opened the book, he found the place where it was written, The Spirit of the Lord is upon me, because he hath anointed me to preach the gospel to the poor; he hath sent me to heal the brokenhearted, to preach deliverance to the captives, and recovering of sight to the blind, to set at liberty them that are bruised, To preach the acceptable year of the Lord. And he closed the book, and he gave it again to the minister, and sat down. And the eyes of all them that were in the synagogue were fastened on him. And he began to say unto them, 'This day is this scripture fulfilled in your ears.'" (Luke 4:16-21)

"For the law was given by Moses, but grace and truth came by Jesus Christ." (John 1:17)

"The woman saith unto him, 'I know that Messias cometh, which is called Christ: when he is come, he will tell us all things.' Jesus saith unto her, 'I that speak unto thee am he.'" (John 4:25-26)

To summarize this, God likes to speak with His children and Jesus enjoys speaking with His brothers and sisters. I have been unable to find anywhere in the Bible that says this part of the relationship, communication, has stopped. On the contrary, personal contact such as face-to-face conversation is necessary for any intimate relationship.

Imagine for a moment that you hear about a person in your work place, or at school if you're a student, who has the same interests as you. You decide that you really want to get to know this person and be a friend to them. What would you do? Would you go to the library to see if they have books about that person to read? Would you go online and look them up in Wikipedia? Would you contact them via Facebook and say, "Do you mind if I follow you?" Of course not! If you did these things and then told the people around you that you were now best friends with this other person, nobody would take you seriously. If this is the case with our relationships with people, how can we just read a book about God and then believe that we have a relationship with Him? There has to be more or it's not real!

In many ways, the Bible reveals that God wants children who choose to love Him, as He loves us. He provided everything we need in order to know Him, gave us choice, showed us that we can't grasp life through our own works, and provided a solution for the fact that we can't reach Him on our own. He did this to prove to us that He loves us (John 3:16). He wants a close, personal relationship with us: for us to know Him, walk with Him daily, and rest in His presence.

To emphasize that our relationship with God is personal, Jesus told His followers that He called them friends. " Henceforth I call you not servants; for the servant knoweth not what his lord doeth: but I have called you friends; for all things that I have heard of my Father I have made known unto you." (John 15:15)

Also, in the story of the Prodigal Son, He showed that what our Father, God, wants most from us is to desire to live with Him and enjoy His presence, now, today! "And he arose, and came to his father. But when he was yet a great way off, his father saw him, and had compassion, and ran, and fell on his neck, and kissed him. And the son said unto him, 'Father, I have sinned against heaven, and in thy sight, and am no more worthy to be called thy son.' But the father said to his servants, 'Bring forth the best robe, and put it on him; and put a ring on his hand, and shoes on his feet: And bring hither the fatted calf, and kill it; and let us eat, and be merry: For this my son was dead, and is alive again; he was lost, and is found.' And they began to be merry." (Luke 15:20-24)

The Bible is an introduction to God. Through the examples it gives us, it is apparent that one of God's main goals for this book is that we would want to have an intimate relationship with Him and to be a part of His family. He will teach us, through His Spirit, and transform us into the image of Jesus! As with other relationships we have, the more time we spend with Him the more blessings we will get out of it! The relationship that He offers is with Him, not with His book.

Chapter 4 - Why is the story of the "Exodus" in the Bible?

Let's take a short journey into one of the greatest stories of all in the Old Testament to see just how much God provided us with guidance on how to know Him and to enjoy a relationship with Him. This is the story of the Children of Israel being freed from slavery in Egypt and being lead to the land that God promised them. God actually first promised it to Abraham over 400 years prior to the beginning of this story. Each step they went through relates to a step we will go through as we grow in Him. We are told in the Bible that this story is filled with examples for us to learn from.

Would you follow a guy with a really bad stutter, who appeared to use magic to try to scare his enemies and impress you? What if he was 80 years old and promised you that God was on his side? What if you were a slave and he promised you freedom? Seems like a stretch, eh? What if you followed him for several years and, although you got to leave the cruel masters you worked under, you never found real freedom? Would you have confidence in following a person like this?

This is a quick summary of how Moses would have looked to the Children of Israel at the time of the Exodus story. God had to provide Moses with a way to prove that it was God that sent him, so that the leaders of the Israelites would believe and go with him. We may look at their story and only notice their bad choices and failures, but they may have been wiser than us. They tested Moses to make sure that God had sent them before they went along with him.

What do we see taking place when people are deciding who to follow today? There are many individuals and religious organizations that make promises to us about what they can deliver. Why should we follow the teachings of individuals or groups today that cannot show that God is the one who sent them and who have no real hope of delivering on their promises? Even more important, who does God want us to follow?

In the first chapter of the book of Exodus, we read that the Children of Israel were crying out to God because the oppression of slavery in Egypt was too much for them to bear. They wanted to be set free from their bondage. God heard their cries and had compassion on them and sent Moses to guide them. But was it God's intention for them to follow Moses?

1Corinthians 10 says that this story was recorded as an example for us and warns us not to be like them, desiring evil, as they did. The book of Hebrews says that they did not believe and couldn't enter His rest. "Wherefore (as the Holy Ghost saith, Today if ye will hear his voice, Harden not your hearts, as in the provocation, in the day of temptation in the wilderness..."

"So I sware in my wrath, They shall not enter into my rest. Take heed, brethren, lest there be in any of you an evil heart of unbelief, in departing from the living God."

"While it is said, 'Today if ye will hear his voice, harden not your hearts, as in the provocation.'"

"So we see that they could not enter in because of unbelief." (Hebrews 3:7-8, 11-12, 15&19)

God wants us to believe Him. When He speaks to us, one intention He has is that our faith be increased. "So then faith cometh by hearing, and hearing by the word of God." He has provided many ways to show us that He is trustworthy. His leading of the Children of Israel out of Egypt was just one of these. This illustrates a variety of ways that He proved Himself. The following are some of the steps God led them through, from this

Exodus story. As I review these I will also discuss the parallels to our lives today.

He started by raising up a deliverer for them, Moses, who as a baby was nearly killed by an evil King. Jesus came as our ultimate deliverer and the enemy also plotted to kill Him through an evil ruler.

God prepared and taught Moses in order to ensure that he would be ready for his role in God's redemptive plan. This included 40 years of tending sheep in the wilderness. God prepared and taught Jesus so He would be ready for His ministry on earth and to accept His destiny on the cross. This included 30 years of learning and maturing before His ministry even started and then 40 days in the wilderness with no food.

God sent Moses to demand that Pharaoh set His people free! Thus He led them out of their bondage to slavery in Egypt. Jesus came to set the captives free and completely defeated the devil on the cross, providing us the way out of slavery to sin.

God used the blood of lambs in Egypt to ensure that the angel of death would pass over all the houses of the Israelites. All they had to do was believe this and take the steps He gave them, to put their faith into action. (This became a feast that has been celebrated ever since by Jews and Christians around the world – Passover.) Jesus shed His blood on the cross for us, at Passover, as our Passover lamb. The result is that God has forgiven us and we are "passed over" for the death we would deserve without His sacrifice. He has traded our death penalty for His life, the abundant life that Jesus promised and paid for.

Up to this point, all that the Israelites had received was a rescue out of slavery. But God had sent them a "Deliverer" in Moses. The mission of a Deliverer is to deliver! Just like when we order something to be sent to our home and a package delivery service transports it. Until the package arrives at the intended destination the delivery is not finished. With the Children of Israel, getting them out of Egypt was only the first step of their deliverance, not deliverance in itself! It is the same for us today. God did not set out to just rescue us from the consequences of our sins and leave us to live a life of survival. He also intends to deliver us to our "Promised Land." More on this promised land in a moment.

If all you ever heard about was that you could be rescued - saved from living in hell for eternity - and it was defined as Salvation, you are missing the best part! God wants to finish the delivery that Jesus paid for in your life. He paid for your delivery and He deserves to receive everything He paid for!

God led the children of Israel out of Egypt toward the place that He had prepared for them, a land flowing with milk and honey. He told them that He would give to them houses, crops and animals that they did not work for. Nehemiah records how He fulfilled this promise. "Their children also multipliedst thou as the stars of heaven, and broughtest them into the land, concerning which thou hadst promised to their fathers, that they should go in to possess it. So the children went in and possessed the land, and thou subduedst before them the inhabitants of the land, the Canaanites, and gavest them into their hands, with their kings, and the people of the land, that they might do with them as they would. And they took strong cities, and a fat land, and possessed houses full of all goods, wells digged, vineyards, and oliveyards, and fruit trees in abundance: so they did eat, and were filled, and became fat, and delighted themselves in thy great goodness." (Nehemiah 9:23-25) This was their Promised Land.

I have a quick question for you, a mini-quiz. Whose idea was it to send the 12 spies into the promised-land when they first arrived at the Jordan River? Was it Moses, checking to see if they people would obey? Was it the people or leaders of the tribes, checking to see with their own eyes if what God had told them was true? Or was it God? Do you know? What were you taught?

(Please see the foot-notes at the end of the chapter for the answer...)

But seriously, would you be surprised to learn that it was God? The reason He did it shows up in the outcome. He wanted them to see that their hearts did not trust Him and that they weren't ready to go in, even though He was ready to lead them in.

They couldn't enter when they first arrived at the Jordan River because they did not trust Him. He told them that He held them out to save their lives because they would be slaughtered by their enemies, unless they fully trusted Him when they entered the land. They overlooked the fact that entering the land, crossing over, was an act of war against the inhabitants there. Those inhabitants knew what it meant and took it seriously! The promised-land was meant to be a place of rest for them, once they trusted God fully.

Today, He leads us toward a place of rest as well (Hebrews 4), which we can only enter by fully placing our trust in Him. This requires us to fully submit to Him, which requires giving up our will to allow His will to guide us instead. Many promises that He made cannot be fulfilled in our lives unless we take this step. Which of these promises are you experiencing? If there are any promises that you are not living in, then submitting to Him is the answer! Jesus explained why this submitting is necessary, several times: "He that loveth his life shall lose it; and he that hateth his life in this world shall keep it unto life eternal." (John 12:25) "But he that is greatest among you shall be your servant." (Matthew 23:11)

The place of rest He wants to take us to is not Heaven, rather it is Heaven on earth, which Jesus referred to as the Kingdom. God doesn't allow us to "cross-over" (enter this place) by accident. Rather, it can only happen when He intentionally allows it, when He knows that we are ready. Entering this Kingdom is where we work out our salvation. It is the necessary step beyond believing Jesus came to save us, just as entering the promised-land was a step beyond following Moses out of Egypt, a step requiring total dependence on Him. I will provide more on this subject in Chapter 7.

Many, if not most, Christians are not aware that entering into His kingdom is available in our lifetime and that it is a declaration of war. But our enemy is aware and takes it very seriously. "For we wrestle not against flesh and blood, but against principalities, against powers, against the rulers of the darkness of this world, against spiritual wickedness in high places." (Ephesians 6:12)

Did God want them to wander in the wilderness for 40 years with no direction? Was this His original purpose for rescuing them from bondage in Egypt? Or was His intent to have them entering the promised-land much sooner? His intent was entering the land in His timing!

They reached the Jordan River just about 2 years after leaving Egypt, the first time, Numbers 9. God used this time to prepare them. It necessarily took a while, rather than just a few days (it can be walked in about 11 days), because He knew that He needed to prepare them for entering the Promised land. It was meant to take long enough for that preparation time, but not too long. Yet, they were not ready for entering when they first arrived. The reasons for this ran deep. Although they had left Egypt, the bondage in their hearts was not gone. They often complained to Moses and told him that they wanted to go back to Egypt, back to slavery! They lived a life of survival, not victory.

God did not intend for their fear to hold them back. Two of the spies who went into the land saw what God had said about the land was true and they believed God. They believed and stated that if God made such an awesome place for them, then surely He would give it to them without them needing to fear! The fact that the rest of the spies did not feel ready to enter Canaan should not have stopped them. It should have confirmed to them that they needed to rely on God.

Does He want us to wander in survival mode or to enter the place of rest once He has prepared us, that place that His victory won for us? His intent is that we enter in His timing and that we fully trust in Him at every step. Yet we often try to make our way on our own, typically failing at trying to survive this world. We even turn back to the things that still have us in bondage, though we pretend they don't. The only way we can be free of them is to turn them over to Him by fully trusting Him and completely submitting. This is the submitting of your will, your selfish desires, to His that I mentioned earlier.

Don't be misled by clichés, "Just trust the Lord with your life, Sister!" "Just give your life to Jesus, Brother!" If you don't really trust Him there is no way you can submit your will to Him. Without submitting your will, you can never follow Him into the place that He has promised you. This place of rest is available here, now, in this life!

When God is ready to lead us into His place of rest, we should not look at the circumstances and check to see if we are able to handle it. We can't handle the battles and that's just the point! God wants to take care of the battles for us, so that we can rest and live in peace. If we're willing to depend on Him, we don't have to worry about whether we are ready because He is!

Some say that our place of rest, our promised land, is Heaven. But look at what actually happened in their promised land? They had wars and battles constantly. This is NOT the Biblical description of Heaven. Heaven is a place of total peace and no suffering. The Promised Land was intended for them to enjoy in this life right here on earth, not after they died. Note that it was God's intent for His people to go directly into the Promised Land when He said it was time.

If the parallel today were Heaven, then why doesn't He just take us up like Elijah, once we come to know Him? No, Heaven is not our promised land. We do not have to wait until we die to begin enjoying what He rescued us to enjoy. His kingdom is our promised land and like the Children of Israel's promised-land, it is available to us to live in now. If we aren't living in it and enjoying it, then it is because we have not entered into His rest.

Even while they wandered in the wilderness, He provided for them. "Thou gavest also thy good spirit to instruct them, and withheldest not thy manna from their mouth, and gavest them water for their thirst. Yea, forty years didst thou sustain them in the wilderness, so that they lacked nothing; their clothes waxed not old, and their feet swelled not." (Nehemiah 9:20-21)

Today He has promised to provide for us if we will let Him (Matthew 6:25-34). This is a promise that seems very seldom pursued and received. Yet, there is no end to what He can fulfill if we take Him up on it!

Once in the Promised Land, God showed them that with His leading they could conquer the land one battle at a time, as long as they relied on Him and obeyed Him. When they disobeyed Him, it caused consequences that were obstacles to their progress because they allowed their enemies to get footholds in their land. In fact, they never fully conquered all of the land because of their disobedience.

Today, He has promised us He has already won the war and our battles will be won, if we trust Him. When we disobey it causes negative consequences, because we allow the enemy a foothold in our thoughts and lives. There are strongholds that the enemy has in our lives, from lies we came to believe before we met Jesus. These can only be conquered with God's help and in His timing. "For the weapons of our warfare are not carnal, but mighty through God to the pulling down of strong holds; Casting down imaginations, and every high thing that exalteth itself against the knowledge of God, and bringing into captivity every thought to the obedience of Christ..." (2Corinthians 10:4-5)

God desires us to believe in and trust Him. Our mutual enemy wants the opposite. Just as he did with Adam and Eve, the devil constantly tries to get us to question what God has said as well as God's motives. He is trying to win over our minds. When we trust God and let Him fight the battles, He wins back ground in our life. We can eventually have complete command of our minds, the battle-field, only if we continue to trust and rely on Him. "I beseech you therefore, brethren, by the mercies of God, that ye present your bodies a living sacrifice, holy, acceptable unto God, which is your reasonable service. And be not conformed to this world: but be ye transformed by the renewing of your mind, that ye may prove what is that good, and acceptable, and perfect, will of God." (Romans 12:1-2)

As they lived in the Promised Land, God let the Children of Israel know that He would not lead them to conquer the land all at once. Instead, He would do it at a pace that was sustainable. He said this was because they needed to grow into it, to be able to hold what they conquered. He knows the right timing and speed for each step of progress in each of our journeys today as well. If we wait on Him for the timing, we will make real progress, which cannot be taken away. We need to grow in order to hold the ground He gives us. Only He knows when we are ready for the next step.

Note! Please don't hear what I am <u>not</u> saying. I said we need to wait on Him to know when to fight battles. I did not say we should sit around and wait for Him to tell us what we need to do all the time, for everything. We already know what to do in many circumstances, because He has given us promises and guidance, both through the Bible and personally/directly. When it comes to battles, the only Biblical example we are given is to wait on Him! There are other circumstances that require waiting on Him as well and He will show you those as you are ready for them.

Throughout the story of the exodus of the Children of Israel from Egypt to the land God promised them, it is evident that God expected His people to follow Him, not a man. This is an important point that He repeats in the New Testament as well.

There are many more parallels from the Exodus journey of the Children of Israel to our lives today. I trust that God will show you more and more as you continue to seek Him! In the coming chapters I will look deeper into some of the issues revealed by this story.

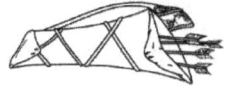

Chapter Five - What is "the Gospel"?

When people ask you "What would you like to hear first, the good news or the bad news?" how do you answer them? Most of us would rather only hear the good news if we admit the truth. We may concede to hear the bad news first, if we have to, just to get it over with.

When you hear the message of the Gospel, does it come across as a good news/bad news message? Is it supposed to be?

The Gospel is at the center of most teaching of Evangelicals around the world. It is important to know how this term is defined? The word actually means good news. So, what's this good news about? Is it about avoiding hell? Is it about salvation? Is it about Jesus dying for us? Is it about receiving forgiveness for our sins? Is it found in John 3:16?

Much teaching about the Gospel is tied to Salvation. The message that goes along with this teaching is that Jesus died to pay for our sins so that we could be saved from Hell and death, the consequences of sin. It is even referred to as the Gospel of Salvation. But where does that name/phrase come from. The only place that phrase is even used in the Bible is a passing comment, not as a title. What then is this good news referring to?

Paul said, "For I am not ashamed of the gospel of Christ: for it is the power of God unto salvation to every one that believeth; to the Jew first, and also to the Greek." (Romans 1:16) This statement conveys the idea that it is very important to know what the Gospel is! If it's really important, wouldn't Jesus have talked about it? Yes, He did. The first recorded words in the Bible that He spoke after His ministry began, after He was baptized by John the Baptizer, were about the Gospel. He said, "The time is fulfilled, and the kingdom of God is at hand: repent ye, and believe the gospel." (Mark 1:15)

Notice that Jesus said, "...repent and believe..." Is this important? Why would He use those terms together? Repent is a highly misunderstood word. It literally means to turn around (away) or to change our thinking to the opposite way of thinking. Jesus was pointing out that we cannot go on thinking the way we have and accept/believe the Gospel message. Jesus knew this because He created us. Jesus was helping to make us aware that in order to receive the truth we have to stop believing any lies that would block it from our minds. For this to happen we have to be willing to be wrong, to admit that some of what we have decided to believe is not based on truth. If we are not willing to be wrong, it is not possible for us to give up a current belief. If we don't give up current beliefs, we won't receive the truth He is trying to reveal to us.

If you haven't repented, then you are living without the truth. The easiest way to tell is to ask yourself, "Am I willing to be wrong?" Be honest, because not knowing the truth will cause you to miss real life!

The book of Mark also says that Jesus went around teaching and proclaiming the Gospel of the Kingdom. Why would this be an important distinction, Gospel of the Kingdom instead of Gospel of salvation? One very good reason is if we think the Gospel is only about being saved from hell, then it is easy to become focused on a future hope. Many who adhere to this teaching believe, "We can be forgiven today, so we can live in Heaven someday." According to this belief, there is something to look forward to someday, but it's not close enough to grasp now. There is no solution to our current circumstances in this belief. The goal is simply to get into Heaven when we die.

The Gospel of the Kingdom is a present-tense Gospel. The message that the Bible provides says God intends for us to have His promises now! These promises provide the solution for every problem we face. The stated goal is for us to be free from what has separated us from God, to be reconciled to God, so that we can truly know Him today!

Jesus even gave us the details of this Kingdom Gospel. Luke 4 contains Jesus' explanation of the Gospel. Beginning in verse 16, Jesus enters the Temple and reads from the book of Isaiah, a prophecy about Himself. He then continues: "The Spirit of the Lord is upon me, because he hath anointed me to preach the gospel to the poor; he hath sent me to heal the brokenhearted, to preach deliverance to the captives, and recovering of sight to the blind, to set at liberty them that are bruised, To preach the acceptable year of the Lord." (Luke 4:18-19)

In summary, He came to "deliver the captives" and He included physical, spiritual and mental freedom. Then He concluded "...To preach the acceptable year of the Lord." By this, He was expressing that it was the appointed time for this gospel to be revealed, the time that this freedom was to be established! He confirmed this as

He went on to tell the crowd in attendance that day that the prophecy in Isaiah was fulfilled in their presence. Not sometime in the future, but right then!

Now that's good news! Since Jesus stated it so clearly, why should we accept anything less?

Some say the Gospel is summarized in John 3:16. Let's take a look at this verse, to see what we find? First, God loves the world. Second, He has just one son and gave Him up on our behalf. Third, if we believe in Him then we can have something called "everlasting life" and do not have to perish (die). Those who adhere to a Salvation Gospel conclude that: 1 - God loves those who love Him or those who accept His son. 2 - Jesus died for those who believe in Him. 3 - Things are going to get great after we die because we get to live in Heaven, some day.

The trouble is, those conclusions don't fit what this verse actually says, nor do they fit other passages that clarify this verse. The verse says that God loves the whole world! Nobody is left out of that statement. When did He send His son? Was it after the world begged for forgiveness? No, it was "while we were still His enemies" as is pointed out in another passage. He loves the whole world, regardless of their response to Him. In another passage Paul tells us that God was "...in

Christ, reconciling the world unto himself." He died for the whole world. Everyone!

In regards to timing of when to expect this thing called eternal life, we see later in the same chapter of John that Jesus points out "He that believeth on the Son hath everlasting life..." (verse 36) That is present tense! We receive everlasting (or eternal) life the moment we receive the Son! Therefore, the term "everlasting life" can't be referring only to living in Heaven after we die.

What in the world is eternal life then? Jesus tells us the answer later in the book of John, "And this is life eternal, that they might know thee the only true God, and Jesus Christ, whom thou hast sent." (John 17:3) Having eternal life is: knowing God and Jesus! We are meant to have this relationship now! There is no need to wait, because truly knowing Him goes hand in hand with living in the Kingdom.

If we allow the Bible to interpret the Bible, then what we find John 3:16 to say is: "God loved every single person in the world so much that He sent His Son to die for all of us, as payment for our sins, so that all of those who place their trust fully in Him will gain Spiritual Life, which is knowing God the Father personally and Jesus Christ His son - now!" Now that is talking about the Gospel of the Kingdom! That really IS good news!

You may ask: What about forgiveness of our sins? Are our sins forgiven? Absolutely! The Father accepted Jesus' payment on the cross and forgave us completely. All that is left is for us to receive that forgiveness, to believe that He did what He said He would do. And that is only the beginning of the promised blessings He has for us. Forgiveness of sins is just the tip of the iceberg of what the Gospel of the Kingdom is about. God intended for us to have all that Jesus paid for. Do NOT settle for a small part of the whole gift!

To get a better picture of some of what this Kingdom Gospel includes for us today, consider some of the statements that Jesus made about what He has delivered, His good news to us:

"I am come that they might have life, and that they might have it more abundantly." (John 10:10b)

"If the Son therefore shall make you free, ye shall be free indeed." (John 8:36)

"These things I have spoken unto you, that in me ye might have peace. In the world ye shall have tribulation: but be of good cheer; I have overcome the world." (John 16:33)

"Fear not, little flock; for it is your Father's good pleasure to give you the kingdom." (Luke 12:32)

"Verily, verily, I say unto you, He that believeth on me, the works that I do shall he do also; and greater works than these shall he do; because I go unto my Father." (John 14:12)

"And these signs shall follow them that believe; In my name shall they cast out devils; they shall speak with new tongues; They shall take up serpents; and if they drink any deadly thing, it shall not hurt them; they shall lay hands on the sick, and they shall recover." (Mark 16:17-18)

Interestingly, Jesus never used fear to attempt to motivate people to like Him or to accept His message of good news about the Kingdom. He only loved them. It worked then and it is still working now, every time it is exercised.

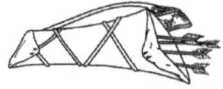

Chapter Six - What does it mean to be "saved"?

Would you be surprised if I told you that it's not what you think? Personally, I think you might be shocked, unless you have picked up hints from what I've already covered. And this is exactly what I'm about to explain: It's not what you may think it is!

But first, let's consider a couple of questions. Is it normal for people to get married so that they can live in separate houses from their spouse and not talk to each other for weeks at a time? Is it typical for people to pay for a new paint job on their car that isn't going to be applied until after they die? If we answer "No" to both of these, why would we accept a salvation that provides no intimate relationship with God and no fulfilled promises until after we die?

Do you ever wonder if you're missing something and perhaps ask, "Is this all there is?" Do you expect more to life on this earth, to the Christian walk, to a relationship with God? Perhaps you're not getting what you should expect to get out of the relationship the Bible talks about.

If you have been taught that being saved means that everything will be great after you die, then I want to suggest that it would be a good idea to get a second opinion! Why not get that second look from the Bible? If getting "saved" is the definitive step to being a Christian, wouldn't the Bible be very clear about it?

When we search for the word saved in the New Testament, we find some interesting things. Jesus told a number of people that "your faith has saved you." This sounds very much like a present tense phrase that He used. Those people actually were physically healed immediately when He made the statement. He also said to other people, "Your faith has healed you..." and at other times, "Your faith has made you well." These statements also were present tense. In one case, Jesus even said that to heal and to forgive sins is the same thing! He even demonstrated this to a group of Pharisees. (Luke 5:20-25)

Interestingly, the same Greek word is used in all of these verses, translated as healed, made whole, saved, etc. That Greek word is Sozo. It also means "delivered" and "made complete."

There are various verses that express what saved/Sozo looks like. Let's read a few of the verses that have this word in them (emphasis added):

"And he said unto him, 'Arise, go thy way: thy faith hath made thee **whole**.'" (Luke 17:19)

"And besought him greatly, saying, My little daughter lieth at the point of death: I pray thee, come and lay thy hands on her, that she may be **healed**; and she shall live." (Mark 5:23)

"And he said to the woman, 'Thy faith hath **saved** thee; go in peace.'" (Luke 7:50)

"They also which saw it told them by what means he that was possessed of the devils was **healed**." (Luke 8:36)

"And the Lord shall deliver me from every evil work, and will **preserve** me unto his heavenly kingdom: to whom be glory for ever and ever. Amen." (2 Timothy 4:18)

By looking at the meaning of the Greek word "Sozo" we find that to be saved includes being healed in all three dimensions: body, soul and spirit. This goes hand-in-hand with the way the Prophet Isaiah (and Jesus) described the Gospel, that Jesus came to set the captives free: physically, mentally and spiritually. (Luke

4) Jesus' explanation of the Gospel matches His use of the word saved!

How do we get from rescued to delivered or Sozo? As I covered in Chapter 4, being delivered speaks about moving something from an origin to a destination. It necessarily includes both components. When the children of Israel were led out of Egypt, that was not deliverance. They were only rescued! God's intention was to place them into the Promised Land, their intended destination! Salvation wasn't fulfilled for them until they were placed into, and delivered to, the Promised Land. Even then, they were not yet completely free. But, by trusting in and depending on God, they began to gain more and more of the land/freedom.

When salvation is taught only as a parallel to leaving Egypt, with no other examples, people are led to think that wandering in their own wilderness today is all there is of the Christian life. Thus it appears that the goal in this life is survival because there is only a rescue here on earth. It is even taught, at times, that the freedom part of salvation only comes after we die. This is not what Jesus taught. Salvation includes the completion of deliverance. He intends to place you into a new location. This new location is the place where we receive freedom here on earth, even experience heaven on earth/the Kingdom of God.

When we accepted Jesus as our Savior did it bring the salvation I'm speaking about? Did it result in freedom and abundant life? Or, are we only able to learn to wander in the wilderness of this world and barely survive? As I mentioned in the previous chapter, most people don't even know that they need to repent when they come to Jesus. This alone is a barrier to receiving the Truth.

As I covered earlier, the Gospel is about much more than this. The Gospel Jesus taught was the Gospel of the Kingdom. With this Gospel, God has given mankind a choice. We may have been taught that this choice is whether or not we want Jesus as our Savior. But it was not our choice to have Him die on the cross, almost 2000 years ago, and for God to accept His sacrifice as full payment for the sins of the world. That was Jesus' choice! Our choice is whether or not we are going to receive the free gift and all the blessings/promises He has offered. That includes being delivered, which is entering the Kingdom. He has allowed us to choose how we live our life, just as the story of the Prodigal son demonstrates. (Luke 15:11-32)

What is this Kingdom? In Chapter 7 I will dig deeper into this question. For now, I will point out a few things that Jesus said about it.   When explaining to His disciples how to pray, He told them to pray in this manner: "Thy kingdom come, Thy will be done in earth, as it is in heaven." (Matthew 6) He also stated: "Verily I say unto you, There be some standing here, which shall not taste of death, till they see the Son of man coming in his kingdom." (Matthew 16:28) He said the kingdom is a distinct entity, apart from Heaven, and we should pray that the Father make the Kingdom like Heaven here on earth. Then He said that some of those who were alive at the time would see Him in His Kingdom before they died! It is clear He was talking about something other than Heaven.

In order to enter His Kingdom, we have to place our trust in Him.   I'm not talking about the traditional phrase, "You have got to trust Jesus with your life." In the traditional Gospel of Salvation, this really means only trusting Him with your future, after you die. That takes no current commitment because it's way off in the future. I'm talking about trusting Him today, with everything that happens. I'm talking about not trying to do everything for yourself, rather letting Him provide as He promised.   We can't do this without submitting our lives fully to Him. This submission on our part allows Him to be Lord.

Most Christians are familiar with the Apostle Paul's statements about the importance of hearing in order to be able to believe. In his letter to the Romans, he said, "... For whosoever shall call upon the name of the Lord shall be saved. How then shall they call on him in whom they have not believed? and how shall they believe in him of whom they have not heard? and how shall they hear without a preacher? And how shall they preach, except they be sent? as it is written, How beautiful are the feet of them that preach the gospel of peace, and bring glad tidings of good things!" (Romans 10:13-15)

This passage is often quoted to show why it is important for people to answer the call to be preachers or missionaries. It is even used as an example of the importance of preaching the gospel. What was Paul talking about when he said "...call upon the name of the Lord?" What does that look like? Paul was not using an idiom of his day. Nor did he mean for us to use another part of the Bible to answer this question. He had actually had just provided an explanation of this in the preceding verses.

These verses are perhaps the most clearly stated message of receiving salvation in the New Testament: "But what saith it? The word is nigh thee, even in thy mouth, and in thy heart: that is, the word of faith, which we preach; That if thou shalt confess with thy mouth the Lord Jesus, and shalt believe in thine heart that God hath raised him from the dead, thou shalt be saved. For with the heart man believeth unto righteousness; and with the mouth confession is made unto salvation." (Romans 10:8-10)   Paul stated that we must confess Jesus as Lord to be saved. He said it is through this confession that we receive salvation. The word confession means to agree with the truth. For Him to be Lord of our life requires that we are fully trusting Him and have submitted to His will, as I pointed out earlier.

He has promised that if we allow Him to be Lord of our lives, we will receive blessings and the many, many, promises that He has prepared ahead of time for us. He has not forced us to allow Him to be Lord of our lives. Instead, He has promised freedom now if we do! Jesus said that we have to give up our life in order to gain it and if we try to hang on to our life we will lose it. (Mark 8:35)

What if the gap between the salvation we may have come to believe in (the Gospel of salvation) and the Salvation that Jesus taught (the Gospel of the Kingdom) can only be filled when He is allowed to be Lord of our life? What if this is the reason that so many of us (the vast majority) have lived our lives without freedom, without abundant life, and without experiencing His promises?

The Bible provides a clear path, the narrow path. The only question left is whether we will choose to let Him lead us on that path?! Will we reject the things that have blocked our path in order to receive all that He has offered? He intended us to walk in His Kingdom daily and have all that He promised! It's time to live! He will prove Himself trustworthy to everyone who trusts Him.

Consider what the Bible says are proofs that we can know we are saved, that we are God's children:

A - The world will know we are Jesus' followers by our love for each other. (John 13:35)

B - God's Holy Spirit confirms to our spirit that we are His children. (Romans 8:16)

C - We're being healed (physically, mentally and physically) delivered from addiction, being made whole, and set free from lies through being truth revealed to us. (Luke 4)

D - We're working out our salvation by learning through experiences in the Kingdom - living it - not striving to find salvation on our own! (Romans 12:1-2)

E - We're seeing God do for us all the things He did for the Children of Israel - and more! (From the books of Exodus through Joshua.)

F - We're doing the works of Jesus and greater works. (John 14:12)

G – We're laying hands on the sick and they are recovering. (Mark 16)

H – We're experiencing real life, abundant life. (John 10:10)

I – We have tribulations and stay peaceful through them, because we trust Him and in return He gives us peace. (John 16:33 and Philippians 4:6-7)

If you recognize that you are missing out on what God had planned for you and you want to know what it's like to experience the freedom that Jesus promised, then the following are the things that open the way to this new life:

Repent of allowing lies stand between you and the truth of God. This turns your mind from believing the lies, to receiving the truth. Being willing to be wrong allows your mind to hear God's Truth.

Believe the Gospel of the Kingdom (putting your trust fully in Him), that Jesus came to earth and paid with His life to set you free from whatever has held you captive and kept you away from God. This includes lies, addictions, fears, sins, doubts and more. Believing the Truth from God sets you free!

Believe that God has raised Jesus from the dead. He is alive and seated at God's right hand. Jesus' death makes Him your Savior. His resurrection guarantees your future life with Him as well.

Confess Jesus as the Lord/Master of your life Agree with Him that you need Him as Lord to lead and guide you, because you cannot do this life without Him. Allow Him to lead the way, His way.

When you talk with God speak as though you are talking to a friend, because that's who you are talking to – the greatest friend you will ever have! Jesus said, "Greater love hath no man than this, that a man lay down his life for his friends." (John 15:13)

You may be reading this and thinking, "But I trusted Jesus, by praying to receive Him..." (or something similar). My question for you is this: Do you really trust Him with your life today? Consider these questions to answer this for yourself:

1. Are you able to be in the world without being like the world? (John 15:19) - Can you describe what that looks like in your life?
2. Have you presented yourself a living sacrifice to the Lord, because this is a reasonable response to what He did for you? (Romans 12:1)
3. Are you allowing your mind to be transformed by being renewing, so you can avoid being

conformed to this world, and so you can find out what God's will is for you? (Romans 12:2)

4. Do you love this world and the things of this world? (1John 2:15-17)

5. Who do you rely on for your next meal, your clothes, and your rent/mortgage payment? (Matthew 6:25-34)

6. Who do you turn to when you're depressed, tired, or sick? Doctors? (Matthew 11:28-30)

7. Do you know how to be free from anxiety? (Philippians 4:6)

8. Are you submitted to God, so that the enemy has no influence in your life? (James 4:7)

9. Do you love your neighbor like you love yourself..."? (Matthew 22:36-39)

10. Do you love other Christians, so the world can see you're a follower of Christ? (John 13:34)

11. Are you willing to give up your life so you can gain it? (Luke 9:24)

All of the questions I've listed above reveal issues that require trust in God, in order to let Him provide a solution to the things that we face daily. Without truly trusting Him, we can't gain victory in these circumstances. Determine to trust Him today and His promises will begin to be fulfilled in your life! He wants you to be free. Trust Him now! That is the key!

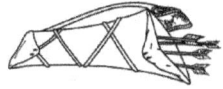

Chapter Seven - What is the "kingdom"?

Did you know one of the reasons that the religious Jews of Jesus' day refused to believe that He could be the Messiah is that they expected the Messiah to be a conquering hero? This Messiah would defeat all their enemies and usher in a new Kingdom where all of His chosen people would then live! Since Jesus came as a baby and didn't fit their image, they just couldn't believe He was who He said He was. And, they are still awaiting this Messiah. This is also one of the main things that evangelical Christians are expecting when Jesus returns, for Him to set up His earthly kingdom and reign here. While they believe that Jesus is the Messiah, they are still waiting for the Kingdom that was prophesied. Doesn't it seem odd that both groups are essentially expecting the same thing?

Well, would you be surprised if I told you that Jesus said the Kingdom is already here and the enemy is defeated! How this could be possible? Check out Jesus' own words:

"But if I cast out devils by the Spirit of God, then the kingdom of God is come unto you." (Matthew 12:28) "Verily I say unto you, There be some standing here, which shall not taste of death, till they see the Son of man coming in his kingdom." (Matthew 16:28)

People living at the time Jesus lived saw the Kingdom arrive! Check out these related passages:

"And he said unto them, 'I beheld Satan as lightning fall from heaven.'" (Luke 10:18)

"Forasmuch then as the children are partakers of flesh and blood, he also himself likewise took part of the same; that through death he might destroy him that had the power of death, that is, the devil..." (Hebrews 2:14)

"He that committeth sin is of the devil; for the devil sinneth from the beginning. For this purpose the Son of God was manifested, that he might destroy the works of the devil." (1John 3:8)

If the Kingdom is here, and has been for almost 2000 years, what does it look like? Some believe and teach that the kingdom spoken of in the New Testament is Heaven. Does this fit the Biblical accounts? A quick reading of some of the verses that mention the Kingdom shows that this is not really possible:

"Thy kingdom come, Thy will be done in earth, as it is in heaven." (Matthew 6:10) They are two clear entities.

"But seek ye first the kingdom of God, and his righteousness; and all these things shall be added unto you." (Matthew 6:33) We are to seek it now, instead of material things.

"And I will give unto thee the keys of the kingdom of heaven: and whatsoever thou shalt bind on earth shall be bound in heaven: and whatsoever thou shalt loose on earth shall be loosed in heaven." (Matthew 16:19) The keys to this kingdom are available now.

"But woe unto you, scribes and Pharisees, hypocrites! for ye shut up the kingdom of heaven against men: for ye neither go in yourselves, neither suffer ye them that are entering to go in." (Matthew 23:13) It's possible to choose to not enter and to hold others out.

"And when he was demanded of the Pharisees, when the kingdom of God should come, he answered them and said, 'The kingdom of God cometh not with observation: Neither shall they say, Lo here! or, lo there! for, behold, the kingdom of God is within you.'" (Luke 17:20-21) It's within us!

"For the kingdom of God is not meat and drink; but righteousness, and peace, and joy in the Holy Ghost." (Romans 14:17) A, concise summary!

"Who hath delivered us from the power of darkness, and hath translated us into the kingdom of his dear Son..." (Colossians 1:13) Delivered – out of – and into.

"And I heard a loud voice saying in heaven, Now is come salvation, and strength, and the kingdom of our God, and the power of his Christ: for the accuser of our brethren is cast down, which accused them before our God day and night." (Revelation 12:10) The Kingdom arrived when Satan was defeated. Now when was that?

There are also many verses that tell us what the Kingdom is like. Here are a few:

"Another parable put he forth unto them, saying, The kingdom of heaven is like to a grain of mustard seed, which a man took, and sowed in his field: Which indeed is the least of all seeds: but when it is grown, it is the greatest among herbs, and becometh a tree, so that the birds of the air come and lodge in the branches thereof.'" (Matthew 13:31-32) It grows and becomes the largest kingdom, supporting life.

"Another parable spake he unto them; The kingdom of heaven is like unto leaven, which a woman took, and hid in three measures of meal, till the whole was leavened.'" (Matthew 13:33) What does the Kingdom do? It spreads, ever increasing, until it has worked its way into everything.

"Again, the kingdom of heaven is like unto treasure hid in a field; the which when a man hath found, he hideth, and for joy thereof goeth and selleth all that he hath, and buyeth that field. Again, the kingdom of heaven is like unto a merchant man, seeking goodly pearls: Who, when he had found one pearl of great price, went and sold all that he had, and bought it." (Matthew 13:44-46) The Kingdom was established when Jesus paid everything to purchase us.

Some believe and teach that the Kingdom is today's organized local churches where believers gather. Reading some of the previously quoted verses shows that this view falls short of the full picture. We do find in the Bible that those who are part of Christ's Church, His body, are definitely part of the Kingdom.

We reviewed earlier that when Jesus started His ministry here on earth, the first thing He was recorded to proclaim to the people was "...The time is fulfilled, and the kingdom of God is at hand: repent ye, and believe the gospel." Then He went around teaching about the Gospel of the Kingdom. He told His disciples that it was with them and would be in them. The word Kingdom is a contraction, made up of two words: King and domain. It is the domain where the King rules. So, where is God's Kingdom? It's wherever He rules. It is in the hearts and lives of those who truly trust in Him. But, He doesn't rule in those who don't trust Him.

In Romans Paul explains that the Kingdom is: "...righteousness, and peace, and joy in the Holy Ghost." (Romans 14:17) This can only be experienced through trust, including total submission. When we trust Him and allow Him to be Lord of our lives, submitting our will to His, then we receive and experience the rest in Him that the book of Hebrews talks about. It is intimacy with the Holy Spirit that gives us righteousness, peace and joy that can be lived and breathed. This is not a figure of speech. It is available to enjoy it in our daily lives!

Hebrews expresses something very important about this rest that is offered in the Kingdom: "Let us therefore fear, lest, a promise being left us of entering into his rest, any of you should seem to come short of it. For unto us was the gospel preached, as well as unto them: but the word preached did not profit them, not being mixed with faith in them that heard it. For we which have believed do enter into rest, as he said, As I have sworn in my wrath, if they shall enter into my rest: although the works were finished from the foundation of the world."
"...For he that is entered into his rest, he also hath ceased from his own works, as God did from his." (Hebrews 4: 1-3&10)

The author of Hebrews points out that we have been given a promise of entering His rest, but we can come short of it, miss it. This problem for the Children of Israel was that the word they heard was not mixed with faith in God. They did not believe that what He told them about their place of rest, the Promised Land, was true. They didn't see the need to stop working to meet their own needs. So, they did not get to enter in.

This can happen to us as well, to Believers today. It's not about working or effort on our part, "...the works were finished from the foundation of the world." There is nothing we can do, in a physical sense, to enter this rest. We have to mix faith with the truth we hear to enter the Kingdom, our place of rest in Him!

And the author of Hebrews goes on to say that those who have believed do enter into rest. He is not speaking of mental acknowledgement, but of placing our total trust and confidence in Christ. This is the Biblical meaning of believe. And then, in verse 10, he points out that we can tell if we have entered the Kingdom when we have stopped working or striving.

Should we then believe that a good way to show faith is to start moving and let God open or shut doors as we go? Does that old saying apply to us: "A ship that's not in motion can't be steered..."? Or should we believe the Bible, "But they that wait upon the LORD shall renew their strength; they shall mount up with wings as eagles; they shall run, and not be weary; and they shall walk, and not faint." (Isaiah 40:31) "Wait on the LORD: be of good courage, and he shall strengthen thine heart: wait, I say, on the LORD." (Psalm 27:14) It is certainly true that if God has told us to move, it would be disobedience to sit still and wait. But moving before we know where He is leading is simply following our own will, not His.

The reason that the Jews of Jesus' day missed this Kingdom, and are still waiting for its arrival today, is that they were expecting a physical Kingdom. It is a Spiritual Kingdom that was prophesied and that Jesus delivered. "Jesus answered, My kingdom is not of this world: if my kingdom were of this world, then would my servants fight, that I should not be delivered to the Jews: but now is my kingdom not from hence." (John 18:36)

To put this Spiritual Kingdom into Heavenly perspective, I offer this question: Why would Jesus want a physical Kingdom? This world is temporary and quickly passing away. The entire existence of it is a mere blip on the timeline of eternity. His Spiritual Kingdom is everlasting. "He shall be great, and shall be called the Son of the Highest: and the Lord God shall give unto him the throne of his father David: And he shall reign over the house of Jacob for ever; and of his kingdom there shall be no end." (Luke 1:32-33)

When Jesus was tempted by the devil, one of the things He was offered was all the kingdoms of the earth. He turned this down! Why accept inferior kingdoms, if you trust the Father is going to give you an everlasting one?!

While Christians teach and believe that Jesus is the Messiah, many miss the fact that His Kingdom was indeed set up here on earth while He was here. They don't know that it's available and that it's God's intention for us to be living in it. Because of that, they are missing all its benefits, including righteousness, peace, and joy in the Holy Spirit. They are also missing true rest, from trusting Him.

When Jesus returns it will not be to set up a physical Kingdom on earth. He only has one Kingdom and it's already here! When He returns He will deliver the Kingdom to the Father! "Then cometh the end, when he shall have delivered up the kingdom to God, even the Father; when he shall have put down all rule and all authority and power." (1Corinthians 15:24)

The Kingdom is God's gift to us here on earth. We can get a taste of what Heaven will be like and can enjoy it now by fully trusting and depending on Christ. It's His way for us to experience the peace He meant for us to have! "Fear not, little flock; for it is your Father's good pleasure to give you the kingdom." (Luke 12:32)

Chapter Eight – What changed because of the Cross?

Imagine that you are a common thief and you live in a country where petty theft is punishable by death. Not just any death, but the most gruesome, painful, slow and tortuous death you could imagine. For people in some countries on earth this is not hard to imagine. One day you get caught by the police, red-handed, with enough merchandise to convict you on the spot. They don't bother with trials in your country. So, they drag you, kicking and screaming, to the place where the execution will take place.

Just as you arrive a stranger steps up and tells the police that he will take your place. They agree and then make you watch as they take this stranger, in your place, to kill him. As he's being prepared for your execution, you recognize him. It's the man you stole from. He didn't do anything wrong. You know that you're the one who is guilty and now you're responsible for his death. Then after it's over they let you go, because your crime has been paid for.

Suddenly, you wake up and realize it was all a dream. But it was SO real - so real you can still feel your heart racing from the fear of the close call.

That's what Jesus did for you! Took your place and paid your debt, in full, on the cross. Only, this is not a dream, this is reality, for all of eternity...

Christians believe that Christ's work on the cross, His complete sacrifice, accomplished everything needed for our sins to be forgiven. This is an amazing gift, we call grace, and we are eternally grateful for it. So, is that all was accomplished? What if there's more? And if you knew, it your entire outlook on the world you live in and who you really are would change? I believe that what the Bible says on this subject may surprise you!

The Old Testament had a lot to say about the fact that a Messiah was going to come. It also recorded much about how life on earth would change due to His efforts. The New Testament opens with the details of His arrival, accompanied by many testimonies by His followers about how much life changed after He arrived. When we look at what has changed, we find many contrasts provided in the Bible between "before" and "after" the cross.

Before: Adam and Eve lost their right to live in the Garden and to their authority to exercise dominion (rule) over the earth.
After: Jesus won back the authority to rule the earth and we are His ambassadors here. (Matthew 28:18)

Before: The temple was a physical building built by Solomon, rebuilt, and eventually destroyed in 70 A.D.
After: Our bodies are the temple of the Holy Spirit. (1Corinthians 3:16)

Before: Obeying the Law was the only hope of receiving relief from physical maladies.
After: Isaiah states that He took our sorrows, iniquities, sicknesses, etc., on Himself on the cross. (Isaiah 53 and Matthew 8:17)

Before: The enemy ruled the earthly, physical realm. On their own, mankind had no way to fight him.
After: Jesus defeated the enemy, on the cross. (1John 3:8) And He won back all power on earth. (Matthew 28:18) Isaiah states that no weapon brought against us will be successful. (Isaiah 54:17) We are more than conquerors! (Romans 8:37) The enemy can still influence, through deception, but has lost all authority.

Before: God's people were fed with manna that fell from the sky, daily.
After: We have Jesus, our bread of life, who satisfies our hunger. (John 6:35)

Before: Obeying the Law and doing sacrifices was expensive.
After: Jesus paid for our needs to be satisfied, for us to be fed spiritually, and He made an everlasting new covenant that only depends on Him. (Isaiah 55:1-3)

Before: The hope of mankind was that a Messiah would come one day and conquer their enemies.
After: Jesus the Messiah conquered our spiritual enemy on the cross, forever. (Isaiah 61:1-3 & Luke 4)

Before: Tithe required a tenth of all that you made.
After: Our tithe is 100%! (Matthew 19:21 & Mark 12:42-44)

Before: God's thoughts are higher than our thoughts and His ways are higher...
After: We have the mind of Christ. (1Corinthians 2:16) We are like Jesus in this world. (1John 4:17) We're being conformed to the image of His son. (Romans 8:29)

Before: People did not know what sin was unless they heard/knew the Law.

After: The Holy Spirit is convicting the world of sin, righteousness and judgment. (John 16:8)

Before: Few people had the Holy Spirit within them. So, there was no conviction of sin in most people.

After: All who believe have the Holy Spirit placed within them. (2Corinthians 1:22)

Before: Obey the Law in order to receive blessings.

After: God has blessed us with every spiritual blessing in Heavenly places, in Christ. (Ephesians 1:3)

Before: Separated from God by disbelief and sin.

After: God was doing a work of reconciling the world to Himself, through Christ, on the cross. (2Corinthians 5:18-19)

Before: God sent prophets to speak to His people.

After: No one else can be the mediator between God and man, but Jesus. (1Timothy 2:5 & Hebrews 1)

Before: People tried to keep the Law to receive forgiveness from others and from God.

After: Whatever sins we forgive will be forgiven, but if we retain them they will be retained. (John 20:23)

Before: All of mankind were slaves to the desires of their fleshly body.
After: God will set us free from these desires, through Jesus. (Romans 7:24-25)

Before: By one man's sin judgment came to everyone.
After: By one man's righteousness, Jesus, the free gift of justification came for everyone. (Romans 5:18)

Before: We were God's enemies.
After: We have peace with God. (Romans 5:1)

Before: We were condemned to death, by the law of death.
After: There is no condemnation for those who are in Christ. And the law of the Spirit of Life has made us free. (Romans 8:1-2)

Before: We had the spirit of bondage to fear.
After: We receive the Spirit of adoption, by our Abba-Father! (Romans 8:15)

Before: We were His enemies.
After: We are His children, joint heirs with Christ. (Romans 8:17)

Before: Mankind was in darkness.
After: We were brought into His light. (1Peter 2:9)

Before: People were on their own to try to keep the Law and fighting to survive.
After: If God is for us, who can stand against us? (Romans 8:31)

Before: The Nation Israel was God's chosen people.
After: Even Gentiles are counted in His family. (Romans 9:25 and Romans 11:24)

Before: Mankind did not know what God had prepared for us. Many things were wrapped in mystery (Isaiah 64:4)
After: God has revealed the mysteries to us by His Spirit! (1Corithians 2:9-10)

Before: We were separated from God.
After: We can boldly enter the holiest place, with confidence in Jesus. (Hebrews 10:19-22)

Before: All of mankind was judged, due to the sin of one man, Adam.
After: God no longer judges anyone, but has left all judgment up to Jesus. (John 5:22) And, when He returns it will not be to judge sin! (Hebrews 9:28 and Revelation 20:12)

Before: Mankind wandered in the wilderness, not even knowing how to survive.

After: We can face various challenges head-on and we are never defeated. (2Corinthians 4:8)

Before: Mankind was condemned by the Law, because it exposed our sin.

After: We are delivered from the law. (Romans 7:6)

One of the best illustrations of how things changed at the cross is the change to God's Temple. The original temple was built to be the place where God dwelt, among His people. But even before the temple was built by Solomon, God gave Moses directions to build a tabernacle for Him in which to dwell among His people. The tabernacle was the temporary/mobile forerunner of the temple. Both the tabernacle and the temple Solomon built were physical pictures, or shadows, of the dwelling that God planned to build for Himself.

In the book of Hebrews, chapter 8 verses 1-5, the author explains that Jesus is now our High Priest, ministering in the true tabernacle that the Lord set up. These verses go on to say that the priests on the earth were ministers in the physical tabernacle, which were a shadow of what was in Heaven and were built after that pattern.

Hebrews 9 explains that Jesus entered the holiest place, which is in God's tabernacle or dwelling place. He entered in through the sacrifice of His own blood. This was not the temple on earth that He entered. Rather, it was God's throne room in Heaven. When He did this, the veil that separated man from God was removed. Matthew explains that this also was manifested in the physical temple. "...and, behold, the veil of the temple was rent in twain from the top to the bottom; and the earth did quake, and the rocks rent..." (Matthew 27:51)

Later, Hebrews goes on to explain that we can now boldly come into the place of God's presence because of Jesus' sacrifice. (Hebrews 10:18-22) Today this place is not a physical location. Instead, it is the center of His true dwelling place that God has built.

If this dwelling place among His people is no longer a physical location, where is it? Paul provided the answer to this question. "What? know ye not that your body is the temple of the Holy Ghost which is in you, which ye have of God, and ye are not your own?" (1Corinthians 6:19) Those who trust Him to be their Lord are His temple, His dwelling place on earth.

Paul also expresses that the entire body of Christ, is being formed together into God's dwelling place. "Now therefore ye are no more strangers and foreigners, but fellowcitizens with the saints, and of the household of God; And are built upon the foundation of the apostles and prophets, Jesus Christ himself being the chief corner stone; In whom all the building fitly framed together groweth unto an holy temple in the Lord: In whom ye also are builded together for an habitation of God through the Spirit." (Ephesians 2:19-22)

This is a description of how His Kingdom has come to us. It is inside those who trust Him as Lord. It is in the form of the dwelling place He inhabits. This was made possible by Jesus' sacrifice on the cross and is manifested in our spiritual being. We can now experience His presence as we learn to live in our spiritual identity, by allowing His Spirit to lead us!

The original tabernacle and temple were the place where God's people came to minister to God, to worship Him, and to make sacrifices to Him for sin. When Jesus made the ultimate sacrifice for all sins, once for all time, the need to continue sacrifices for sin was ended. Today the temple inside of us is our place to minister to God by worshipping Him and giving Him our sacrifices of praise. (Hebrews 13:15)

Worshiping God is not the only purpose for God's dwelling place. God had another very important purpose for His temple. He told His people that "...for mine house shall be called an house of prayer for all people." (Isaiah

56:7) Jesus found that the physical temple in Jerusalem had come to be used for other purposes. He proclaimed that this was not God's plan! "And Jesus entered the temple and drove out all who sold and bought in the temple, and he overturned the tables of the money-changers and the seats of those who sold pigeons. He said to them, " And Jesus went into the temple of God, and cast out all them that sold and bought in the temple, and overthrew the tables of the moneychangers, and the seats of them that sold doves, And said unto them, It is written, My house shall be called the house of prayer; but ye have made it a den of thieves.'" (Matthew 21:12-13) This house of prayer is now the temple within us.

Conclusion: Everything about us - who we are, what our role is here on earth, and what we can accomplish - changed at the cross! It is much too easy to look right past this truth, when we're focused on the physical realm instead of the Spiritual. Paul pointed out, "Therefore if any man be in Christ, he is a new creature: old things are passed away; behold, all things are become new." (2Corinthians 5:17) He was speaking of our identity becoming new. Who we are has become new because our spirit was dead and is now alive! According to Paul's outlook, we are spiritual beings. This means our identity has changed from the physical being that we were when we were first born, to a different type of being when we were born again. Our spirit was born, awakened. Being born again does not mean that our body is born twice. It means that our spirit has come to life!

A part of the adventure of the Christian life is to learn what this life, as a spiritual being, is like. Just like when we were physical babies, we need to learn how to do everything from the beginning. This requires practice and experimentation. We have to learn:
- How to eat = to take in the truth that is needed to transform our minds, from physical to spiritual or heaven focused thinking.
- How to walk by faith = trusting the Truth that God tells us instead of what our eyes tell us.
- How to talk = to speak the Truth in love.
- Who we are = let the Holy Spirit guide us and teach us all things.

Those who never learn about their new spiritual identity, which is meant to be experienced here on earth, miss out on growing up in Him. Instead, they remain spiritual babies their whole life on earth, not growing in the intimate relationship He wants us to have with Him.

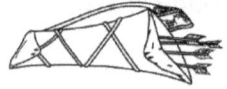

Chapter Nine – Are we to believe the Bible or our own misbeliefs?

It is much easier to accept what people are telling us when it agrees with our own beliefs. Conversely, it is too easy to react and argue with someone when we are hearing something that appears to be at odds with our beliefs. We might even consider their statements outrageous! Why should we even listen to people who don't agree with us? After all, what we have learned up to now is the truth isn't it? Or is it?

Outrageous statements -

The Bible has many statements in it that are either outrageous, because they disagree with our chosen theology, or they are life-giving and liberating! Which one will they be for you? (emphasis added)

" Herein is our love made perfect, that we may have boldness in the day of judgment: because <u>as he is, so are we in this world</u>." (1John 4:17)

"For as by one man's disobedience <u>many</u> were made sinners, so by the obedience of one shall <u>many</u> be made righteous." (Romans 5:19)

" And these signs shall follow <u>them that believe</u>; In my name shall they cast out devils; they shall speak with new tongues; They shall take up serpents; and if they drink any deadly thing, it shall not hurt them; they shall lay hands on the sick, and they shall recover." (Mark 16:17-18)

"Blessed be the God and Father of our Lord Jesus Christ, who hath <u>blessed us with all spiritual blessings</u> in heavenly places in Christ..." (Ephesians 1:3)

"Now unto him that is able to do exceeding abundantly above all that we ask or think, according to the power <u>that worketh in us</u>..." (Ephesians 3:20)

"Verily I say unto you, Among them that are born of women there hath not risen a greater than John the Baptist: notwithstanding he that is least in the kingdom of heaven is <u>greater than he</u>." (Matthew 11:11)

"And whatsoever ye do, do it heartily, as to the Lord, and not unto men; Knowing that of the Lord <u>ye shall receive the reward</u>

of the inheritance: for ye serve the Lord Christ." (Colossians 3:23-24)

"And I will give unto thee the keys of the kingdom of heaven: and whatsoever thou shalt bind on earth shall be bound in heaven: and whatsoever thou shalt loose on earth shall be loosed in heaven." (Matthew 16:19)

"Whose soever sins ye remit, they are remitted unto them; and whose soever sins ye retain, they are retained." (John 20:23)

"...That at the name of Jesus every knee should bow, of things in heaven, and things in earth, and things under the earth; And that every tongue should confess that Jesus Christ is Lord, to the glory of God the Father." (Philippians 2:10-11)

"And when he putteth forth his own sheep, he goeth before them, and the sheep follow him: for they know his voice." & "I am the good shepherd: the good shepherd giveth his life for the sheep." (John 10:4&11)

"...And hath made us kings and priests unto God and his Father; to him be glory and dominion for ever and ever. Amen." (Revelation 1:6)

"And heal the sick that are therein, and say unto them, The kingdom of God is come nigh unto you." (Luke 10:9)

"Death and life are in the power of the tongue: and they that love it shall eat the fruit thereof." (Proverbs 18:21)

"And he is the propitiation for our sins: and not for ours only, but also for the sins of the whole world." & "I write unto you, little children, because your sins are forgiven you for his name's sake." (1John 2:2&12)

"But ye are a chosen generation, a royal priesthood, an holy nation, a peculiar people; that ye should shew forth the praises of him who hath called you out of darkness into his marvellous light..." (1Peter 2:9)

"But if the Spirit of him that raised up Jesus from the dead dwell in you, he that raised up Christ from the dead shall also quicken your mortal bodies by his Spirit that dwelleth in you." (Romans 8:11)

"But God, who is rich in mercy, for his great love wherewith he loved us, Even when we were dead in sins, hath quickened us together with Christ, (by grace ye are saved;) And hath raised us up together, and made us sit together in heavenly places in Christ Jesus..." (Ephesians 2:4-6)

"To whom God would make known what is the riches of the glory of this mystery among the Gentiles; which is Christ in you, the hope of glory." (Colossians 1:27)

"For <u>all the promises of God in him are yea, and in him Amen,</u> unto the glory of God by us." (2Corinthians 1:20)

"But he that is joined unto the Lord <u>is one spirit.</u>" (1Corinthians 6:17)

Common Misbeliefs –

In Jesus' day, very few people had a copy of Scripture of their own. Those who did not have Scripture to read typically relied on the spoken word or the beliefs of others. As I pointed out in a previous chapter, in order to know what the truth is we have to that it came from God. Thus Jesus spent a lot of His time with His disciples correcting their misbeliefs about who He was and what He came to do.

Today many misbeliefs are spoken daily in Christian circles even though God is still communicating with His children and most Christians have multiple Bibles in their homes. Misbeliefs can proliferate when people don't know what God has said on a topic. Rather than taking time to check to see if what we have heard is in the Bible, we may pass it on to others. When we hear something that sounds right from someone we know and trust, it may seem silly to question whether it is correct. When we don't check what God has to say on a subject, we leave ourselves open to accepting a misbelief.

Most people would not characterize misbeliefs as lies, especially when they seem to agree with their own belief system. However, misbeliefs are by definition untrue and therefore are actually based in a lie. When we accept lies, it keeps us from being free. God wants us to be free and the Bible will correct misbeliefs!

Finding the truth that resolves a misbelief is similar to debunking a myth. Here are a few examples of common misbeliefs in Christian circles, contrasted with Biblical statements on the respective subject.

Misbelief: We must love the sinner, but hate the sin. Bible: Jesus said to forgive the sin and love the sinner. "For if ye forgive men their trespasses, your heavenly Father will also forgive you: But if ye forgive not men their trespasses, neither will your Father forgive your trespasses." (Matthew 6:14-15) It appears that there is a good reason for us to forgive the sin! God has forgiven our sins. He has asked that we extend that mercy to others and has included a promise when we do.

Misbelief: You have to ask Jesus into your heart to be saved. Bible: Jesus said, "...Whosoever will come after me, let him deny himself, and take up his cross, and follow me."

(Mark 8:34b) The place to start is to follow <u>Him</u>, which requires submitting our will to His will.

Misbelief: Jesus is the only way to Heaven. Bible: Jesus said, "I am the way, the truth, and the life: no man cometh unto the Father, but by me." (John 14:6) He is the only way to God, the Father. Heaven is <u>not</u> the goal of the Christian life. The goal is intimacy with our Heavenly Father!

Misbelief: To be absent from the body is to be face to face with the Lord. Bible: This is a misquote of Paul. What he actually said was: "We are confident, I say, and willing rather to be absent from the body, and to be present with the Lord." (2Corinthians 5:8) He was not talking about what happens to us at death.

Misbelief: God has stopped talking to His children, since the Bible is complete. Bible: Jesus said, "It is written, Man shall not live by bread alone, but by every word that proceedeth out of the mouth of God." (Matthew 4:4) The Bible does not claim to contain all of God's words. The "word" mentioned in verse 4 is referring to a word that comes now, directly from God to you!

Misbelief: Healing doesn't happen anymore and we can only expect to see small miracles. Bible: Jesus said, "Verily, verily, I say unto you, He that believeth on me, the works that I do shall he do also; and greater works than these shall he do; because I go unto my Father." (John 14:12) The issue here is not what the meaning of the word "greater" is, rather the focus is that those who believe will do this! Those who don't believe won't. Which group do you want to be in?

Misbelief: God is judging the world, nations and individuals for their sins/crimes/etc. Bible: Jesus said, "For the Father judgeth no man, but hath committed all judgment unto the Son..." (John 5:22) How could God forgive sin at the cross and then keep on judging?

Misbelief: God's children are never going to experience tribulation, because He said, "I have not destined you for wrath..." Bible: Jesus said, "These things I have spoken unto you, that in me ye might have peace. In the world ye shall have tribulation: but be of good cheer; I have overcome the world." (John 16:33) We have reason to rejoice, He has overcome the world. No matter what is coming, we know who wins!

Misbelief: People who don't live as God intended are our enemies and we have to stop them no matter what it takes. This includes people who live alternate lifestyles and those who are not pro-life. Bible: Jesus said, "But I say unto you, Love your enemies, bless them that curse you, do good to them that hate you, and pray for them which despitefully use you, and persecute you..." (Matthew 5:44) And Paul said, "For we wrestle not against flesh and blood, but against principalities, against powers, against the rulers of the darkness of this world, against spiritual wickedness in high places." (Ephesians 6:12) The only battle we have is with the enemy of our souls! And, that battle belongs to the Lord.

Misbelief: I have the right to sue anyone who wrongs me. Bible: Jesus said, "And if any man will sue thee at the law, and take away thy coat, let him have thy cloak also." (Matthew 5:40) People are not the cause of our problems. They need our love!

Misbelief: It's a good idea to get a receipt for your giving to a fund for the poor, because then you can get a tax deduction. Bible: Jesus said, "But when thou doest alms, let not thy left hand know what thy right hand doeth: That thine alms may be in secret: and thy Father which seeth in secret himself shall reward thee openly." (Matthew 6:3-4) God will reward us if we give, without seeking a reward from men. This is giving with no expectation of anything in return from those who we give to. Otherwise, we are walking away from His blessings, which He promises are better. What if God asked you to give in the same manner to other causes? Would you be willing to give up a tax deduction for His rewards?

Misbelief: We aren't supposed to ever seek treasures, because wealth is a bad thing. Bible: Jesus said, "But lay up for yourselves treasures in heaven, where neither moth nor rust doth corrupt, and where thieves do not break through nor steal: For where your treasure is, there will your heart be also." (Matthew 6:20-21) Paul did warn us about the love of money (1Timothy 6:10) and Jesus pointed out that it is hard for the rich to give up what they have for His sake. (Matthew 19)   However, God gives wealth to be used for His kingdom and we are His stewards.   The issue is whether we will invest in building the Kingdom with what He gives us, as He guides.

Misbelief: God helps those who help themselves. Bible: Jesus said, "But seek ye first the kingdom of God, and his righteousness; and all these things shall be added unto you." (Matthew 6:33) By leaving our needs in His hands, we allow Him to work out the details in His own way. If not, we miss the blessings of seeing this promise fulfilled.

Misbelief: We have to study the Bible intently and learn from theologians and others who have gone before us, in order to know how God wants us to live. Bible: Jesus said, "Howbeit when he, the Spirit of truth, is come, he will guide you into all truth: for he shall not speak of himself; but whatsoever he shall hear, that shall he speak: and he will shew you things to come." (John 16:13)   When we insist on trying to find Truth on our own, from other sources, we stop God's Holy Spirit from fulfilling this role in our lives.

Misbelief: We must listen to great teachers to be able to learn what the Bible means. Bible: Jesus said, "But be not ye called Rabbi: for one is your Master, even Christ; and all ye are brethren." (Matthew 23:8) & "But the Comforter, which is the Holy Ghost, whom the Father will send in my name, he shall teach you all things, and bring all things to your remembrance, whatsoever I have said unto you." (John 14:26) He is our real teacher and will use many methods and sources to teach us, if we seek Him.

Misbelief: Leaders in the local gatherings can only lead by living above the common people. Bible: Jesus said, "But he that is greatest among you shall be your servant." (Matthew 23:11) The most important role is to serve, which is to lift others up. Jesus said that He did not come to be served, but to serve.

Misbelief: If it didn't happen in the Bible, don't expect to experience it in your life. Bible: An angel told Mary that she would become pregnant, even though she had never had intimate contact with a man. Despite the fact that this had never happened to anyone in Scripture, she believed the angel! (Luke 1) Zachariah, John the Baptist's Father, was told by an angel that his wife would have a baby and they were to name him John. Zachariah rejected the name because it was not a name used in their family. He was struck dumb from that day, until the baby was born. (Luke 1) Which experience would you rather have? Both situations required trusting God, rather than misbeliefs.

Misbelief: Our group has the truth about God and the Bible, like no other group. Bible: Jesus prayed for the unity of all those who would choose to follow Him. (John 17) & "And John answered him, saying, Master, we saw one casting out devils in thy name, and he followeth not us: and we forbad him, because he followeth not us. But Jesus said, Forbid him not: for there is no man which shall do a miracle in my name, that can lightly speak evil of me. For he that is not against us is on our part." (Mark 9:38-40) The goal is to build His Kingdom in unity with Him and other believers. Competition is the opposite of unity.

Misbelief: The Bible is the word of God. Bible: When referring to God's book, the authors use the term "Scripture" in most instances. John 1 says the "Word" is Jesus. And to be even clearer, consider this verse in Revelation "And he was clothed with a vesture dipped in blood: and his name is called The Word of God." (Revelation 19:13) This phrase should keep our focus on Jesus, not His book.

Misbelief: We should give advice from our past to people experiencing anxiety, expecting to help them be free from the stresses of this life. Bible: "Come unto me, all ye that labour and are heavy laden, and I will give you rest. Take my yoke upon you, and learn of me; for I am meek and lowly in heart: and ye shall find rest unto your souls. For my yoke is easy, and my burden is light." (Matthew 11:28-30) & "Be careful for nothing; but in every thing by prayer and supplication with thanksgiving let your requests be made known unto God. And the peace of God, which passeth all understanding, shall keep your hearts and minds through Christ Jesus." (Philippians 4:6-7) Man's methods to find peace are all based on self-help principles.

Misbelief: Fear is a natural human reaction to difficult external forces. Bible: 1John says that if we fear we don't know God. Paul said, "For ye have not received the spirit of bondage again to fear; but ye have received the Spirit of adoption, whereby we cry, Abba, Father." (Romans 8:15) Every child of God has been given a new, reborn spirit so we can know love and live life trusting Him without fear.

Misbelief: God said He would never give His glory to man. Bible: What Isaiah wrote about this was " I am the LORD: that is my name: and my glory will I not give to another, neither my praise to graven images." (Isaiah 42:8) This is God saying He will not give idols His glory. In the New Testament Paul said "...and whom he justified, them he also glorified." (Romans 8:30b) This is speaking about people who believe and follow Him.

Misbelief: God has promised to never give us trials or tests that are more than we can handle. Bible: Paul said, "There hath no temptation taken you but such as is common to man: but God is faithful, who will not suffer you to be tempted above that ye are able; but will with the temptation also make a way to escape, that ye may be able to bear it." (1Corinthians 10:13) This promise is about temptations, not about trials and tests. In regards to trials and tests, He has promised that He won't give us anything that <u>He</u> can't handle. "And we know that all things work together for good to them that love God, to them who are the called according to his purpose." (Romans 8:28)

Summary: If a statement or teaching doesn't agree with biblical truth, it may simply be a misbelief. People are led to place their trust in something other than God when they believe the lies that are behind misbeliefs. God wants us to receive the blessings that come from placing our trust in Him alone. The first step to receive them is learn and believe the promises that He has given us, rather than the misbeliefs we accepted when we didn't know where to find the truth.

One common way we fall into accepting misbeliefs is by taking several verses, a single verse, or even part of a verse by itself, out of context. It is always important to take the context of a verse into consideration. This can be done by reading a portion of the Bible before and after that verse to get a more complete picture.

Learning and believing the truth about God's promises is the difference between life and survival. God wants to renew your mind as you get to know Him. He will do this at a pace that you are ready for.

Afterword:

In this book I have provided an introduction to a view of the Gospel that is right-side-up, taking the Bible at face value. It was not my intention to provide the answers to all the possible questions about the Gospel, although you may have found some answers in these pages. God has promised to do that for you.

If you are interested in knowing more, you will find it. God has promised, "If you seek Me with all your heart, you will find Me."

Once you know that you can expect to hear God, and you know how to hear Him, you have the key that will lead to the Kingdom living you have been searching for. You don't need anything else from man in order to know God. He has placed the ability to know Him inside you. One of the most popular types of books on the best-sellers lists year after year is self-help books. People love them. You can find self-help books on any topic and learn how to do almost anything by yourself. The Bible is not a self-help book! Jesus did everything we need on the cross. Now He is inviting you to live out your life in His kingdom. All He is asking you to do is trust Him. He has given us His Holy Spirit to guide us along the way.

If for some reason the idea of Kingdom living doesn't sound interesting to you, I want you to know that I am praying for you. The enemy of your soul does not want you to enjoy the life that Jesus died to give to you. God, however, is waiting and watching for you to call out to Him and ask for that which only He can give:

> "Ho, every one that thirsteth, come ye to the waters, and he that hath no money; come ye, buy, and eat; yea, come, buy wine and milk without money and without price. Wherefore do ye spend money for that which is not bread? and your labour for that which satisfieth not? hearken diligently unto me, and eat ye that which is good, and let your soul delight itself in fatness. Incline your ear, and come unto me: hear, and your soul shall live; and I will make an everlasting covenant with you, even the sure mercies of David."
> (Isaiah 55:1-3)

God will bless you on your journey!